The Christian
A Story Third Book
The Devil's Acre

by

Hall Caine

The Christian
A Story Third Book The Devil's Acre
by Hall Caine

ISBN: 978-93-68094-96-8

Published by

DOUBLE 9 BOOKS

2/13-B, Ansari Road
Daryaganj, New Delhi – 110002
info@double9books.com
www.double9books.com
Tel. 011-40042856

This book is under public domain

ABOUT THE AUTHOR

Hall Caine was a British novelist, dramatist, short story writer, poet, and critic in the late nineteenth and early twentieth centuries. Caine enjoyed exceptional fame throughout his lifetime. He published fifteen novels on infidelity, divorce, domestic abuse, illegitimacy, infanticide, religious prejudice, and women's rights, becoming a worldwide literary celebrity and selling 10 million copies. Caine was the highest-paid novelist of his day. The Eternal City is the first novel to sell more than one million copies globally. Caine moved to the Isle of Man in 1895 and served in the Manx House of Keys, the island's lower house of parliament, from 1901 to 1908. Caine was elected President of the Manx National change League in 1903 and chaired the Keys' Committee, which drafted the 1907 constitutional change petition. Caine received the Freedom of the Borough of Douglas on the Isle of Man in 1929. Caine traveled to Russia in 1892 on behalf of the persecuted Jews. Caine traveled to the United States and Canada in 1895, representing the Society of Authors, where he successfully negotiated and obtained significant international copyright concessions from the Dominion Parliament.

CONTENTS

CHAPTER I

Behind Buckingham Palace there is a little square of modest houses standing back from the tide of traffic and nearly always as quiet as a cloister. At one angle of the square there is a house somewhat larger than the rest but just as simple and unassuming. In the dining-room of this house an elderly lady was sitting down to lunch alone, with the covers laid for another at the opposite end of the table.

"Hae ye the spare room ready, Emma?"

"Yes, ma'am," said the maid.

"And the sheets done airing? And baith the pillows? And the pillow-slips—and everything finished?"

The maid was answering "Yes" to each of these questions when a hansom cab came rattling up to the front of the house, and the old lady leaped out of her seat.

"It's himself!" she cried, and she ran like a girl to the hall.

The door had been opened before she got there, and a deep voice was saying, "Is Mrs. Callender — —"

"It's John! My gracious! It's John Storm!" the old woman cried, and she lifted both hands as if to fling herself into his arms.

"My guidness, laddie, but you gave poor auld Jane sic a start! Expected ye? To be sure we expected you, and terribly thrang we've been all morning making ready. Only my daft auld brain must have been a wee ajee. But," smiling through her tears, "has a body never a cheek, that you must be kissing at her hand? And is this your dog?" looking down at the bloodhound. "Welcome? Why, of course it's welcome. What was I saying the day, Emma? 'I'd like fine to have a dog,' didn't I? and here it is to our hand.—Away with ye, James, man, and show Mr. Storm to his room, and then find a bed for the creature somewhere. Letters for ye, laddie? Letters enough, and you'll find them on the table upstairs. Only, mind ye, the lunch is ready, and your fish is getting cold."

John Storm opened his letters in his room. One of them was from his uncle, the Prime Minister: "I rejoice to hear of your most sensible resolution.

Come and dine with me at Downing Street this day week at seven o'clock. I have much to say and much to ask, and I expect to be quite alone."

Another was from his father: "I am not surprised at your intelligence, but if anything could exceed the folly of going into a monastery it is the imbecility of coming out of it. The former appears to be a subject of common talk in this island already, and no doubt the latter will soon be so."

John flinched as at a cut across the face and then smiled a smile of relief. Apparently Glory was writing home wherever she was, and there was good news in that, at all events. He went downstairs.

"Come your way in, laddie, and let me look at ye again. Man, but your face is pale and your bonnie eyes are that sunken. But sit ye down and eat. They've been starving ye, I'm thinking, and miscalling it religion. It's enough to drive a reasonable body to drink. Carnal I am, laddie, and I just want to put some flesh on your bones. Monks indeed! And in this age of the world too! Little Jack Horners sitting in corners and saying, 'Oh, what a good boy am I!'"

John defended his late brethren. They were holy men; they lived a holy life; he had not been good enough for their company. "But I feel like a sailor home from sea," he said; "tell me what has happened."

"Births, marriages, and deaths? I suppose ye're like the lave of the men, and think nothing else matters to a woman. But come now, more chicken? No? A wee bitty? Aye, but ye're sair altered, laddie! Weel, where can a body begin?"

"The canon—how is he?"

"Fine as fi'pence. Guid as ever in the pulpit? Aye, but it's a pity he doesna' bide there, for he's naething to be windy of when he comes out of it. Deacon now, bless ye, or archdeacon, and some sic botherment, and his daughter is to be married to yon slip of a curate with the rabbit mouth and the heather legs. Weel, she wasna for all markets, ye ken."

"And Mrs. Macrae?"

"Gone over to the angels. Dead? Nae, ye're too expecting altogether. She's got religion though, and holds missionary meetings in her drawing-room of a Monday, and gives lunches to actor folk of a Sunday, and now a poor woman that's been working for charity and Christianity all her days has no chance with her anyway."

"And Miss Macrae?"

"Poor young leddy, they're for marrying her at last! Aye, to that Ure man, that lord thing with the eyeglass. I much misdoubt but her heart's been somewhere else, and there's ane auld woman would a hantle rather have heard tell of her getting the richt man than seeing the laddie bury hisel' in a monastery. She's given in at last though, and it's to be a grand wedding they're telling me. Your Americans are kittle cattle—just the Jews of the West seemingly, and they must do everything splendiferously. There are to be jewels as big as walnuts, and bouquets five feet in diameter, and a rope of pearls for a necklace, and a rehearsal of the hale thing in the church. Aye, indeed, a rehearsal, and the 'deacon, honest man, in the middle of the magnificence."

John Storm's pale face was twitching. "And the hospital," he said, "has anything happened there—?"

"Nothing."

"No other case such as the one——"

"Not since yon poor bit lassie."

"Thank God!"

"It was the first ill thing I had heard tell of her for years, and the nurses are good women for all that. High-spirited? Aye; but dear, bright, happy things, to think what they have to know and to be present at! Lawyers, doctors, and nurses see the worst of human nature, and she'd be a heartless woman who'd no make allowances for them, poor creatures!"

John Storm had risen from the table with a flushed face, making many excuses. He would step round to the hospital; he had questions to ask there, and it would be a walk after luncheon.

"Do," said Mrs. Callender, "but remember dinner at six. And hark ye, hinny, this house is to be your hame until you light on a better one, so just sleep saft in it and wake merrily. And Jane Callender is to be your auld auntie until some ither body tak's ye frae her, and then it'll no be her hand ye'll be kissing for fear of her wrinkles, I'm thinking."

The day was bright, the sun was shining, and the streets were full of well-groomed horses in gorgeous carriages with coachmen in splendid liveries going to the drawing-room in honour of the royal birthday. As John went by the palace the approaches to it were thronged, the band of the Household Cavalry was playing within the rails, and officers in full-dress uniform, members of the diplomatic service with swords and cocked hats, and ladies in gorgeous brocades carrying bouquets of orchids and wearing tiaras of diamonds and large white plumes were filing through the gate toward the throne-room.

The hospital looked strangely unfamiliar after so short an absence, and there were new faces among the nurses who passed to and fro in the corridors. John asked for the matron, and was received with constrained and distant courtesy. Was he well? Quite well. They had a resident chaplain now, and being in priest's orders he had many opportunities where death was so frequent. Was he sure he had not been ill? John understood—it was almost as if he had come out of some supernatural existence, and people looked at him as if they were afraid.

"I came to ask if you could tell me anything of Nurse Quayle?"

The matron could tell him nothing. The girl had gone; they had been compelled to part with her. Nothing serious? No, but totally unfit to be a nurse. She had some good qualities certainly—cheerfulness, brightness, tenderness—and for the sake of these, and his own interest in the girl, they had put up with inconceivable rudeness and irregularities. What had become of her? She really could not say. Nurse Allworthy might know—and the matron took up her pen.

John found the ward Sister with the house doctor at the bed of a patient. She was short, even curt, said over her shoulder she knew nothing about the girl, and then turned back to her work. As John passed out of the ward the doctor followed him and hinted that perhaps the porter might be able to tell him something.

The porter was difficult at first, but seeing his way clearer after a while he admitted to receiving letters for the nurse and delivering them to her when she called. That was long ago, and she had not been there since New Year's Eve. Then she had given him a shilling and said she would trouble him no more.

John gave him five shillings and asked if anybody ever called for her. Yes, once. Who was it? A gentleman. Had he left his name? No, but he had said he would write. When was that? A day or two before she was there the last time.

Drake! There could not be a shadow of a doubt of it. John Storm looked at the clock. It was 3:45. Then he buttoned his coat and crossed the street to the park with his face in the direction of St. James's Street.

Horatio Drake had given a luncheon in his rooms that day in honour of Glory's first public appearance. The performance was to come off at night, but in the course of the morning there had been a dress rehearsal in the *salon* of the music hall. Twenty men and women, chiefly journalists and artists, had assembled there to get a first glimpse of the *débutante*, and cameras had lurked behind *portières* and in alcoves to catch her poses, her expressions, her fleeting smiles, and humorous grimaces. Then the company had adjourned to Drake's chambers. The luncheon was now over, the last guest had gone, and the host was in his dining-room alone.

Drake was standing by the chimney-piece holding at arm's length a pencil sketch of a woman's beautiful face and lithe figure. "Like herself—alive to the fingertips," he thought, and then he propped it against the pier-glass.

There was a sound of the opening and closing of the outer door downstairs, and Lord Robert entered the room. He looked heated, harassed, and exhausted. Shaking out his perfumed pocket handkerchief, he mopped his forehead, drew a long breath, and dropped into a chair.

"I've done it," he said; "it's all over."

Polly Love had lunched with the company that day, and Lord Robert had returned home with her in order to break the news of his approaching marriage. While the girl had been removing her hat and jacket he had sat at the piano and thumbed it, hardly knowing how to begin. All at once he had said, "Do you know, my dear, I'm to be married on Saturday?" She had said nothing at first, and he had played the piano furiously. Heavens, what a frame of mind to be in! Why didn't the girl speak? At last he had looked round at her, and there she stood grinning, gasping, and white as a ghost. Suddenly she had begun to cry. Good God, such crying! Yes, it was all over. Everything had been settled somehow.

"But I'll be in harder condition before I tackle such a job again."

There was silence for a moment. Drake was leaning on the mantelpiece, his legs crossed, and one foot beating on the hearth-rug. The men were ashamed, and they began to talk of indifferent things. Smoke? Didn't mind. Those Indian cigars were good. Not bad, certainly.

At length Drake said in a different voice, "Cruel but necessary, Robert—necessary to the woman who is going to be your wife, cruel to the poor girl who has been."

Lord Robert rose to his feet impatiently, stretched his arm, and shot out his striped cuff and walked to and fro across the room.

"Pon my soul, I believe I should have stuck to the little thing but for the old girl, don't you know. She's made such a good social running lately—and then she's started this evangelical craze too. No, Polly wouldn't have suited her book anyhow."

Silence again, and then further talk on indifferent things.

"Wish Benson wouldn't sweep the soda water off the table." "Ring for it." "The little thing really cares for me, don't you know. And it isn't my fault, is it? I had to hedge. Frank, dear boy, you're always taunting me with the treadmill we have to turn for the sake of society, and so forth, but with debts about a man's neck like a millstone, what could one do——"

"I don't mean that you're worse than others, old fellow, or that sacrificing this one poor child is going to mend matters much——"

"No, it isn't likely to improve my style of going, is it?"

"But that man John Storm was not so far wrong, after all, and for this polygamy of our 'lavender-glove tribe' the nation itself will be overtaken by the judgment of God one of these days."

Lord Robert broke into a peal of derisive laughter. "Go on," he cried. "Go on, dear boy! It's funny to hear you, though—after to-day's proceedings too"; and he glanced significantly around the table.

Drake brought down his fist with a thump on to the mantelpiece. "Hold your tongue, Robert! How often am I to tell you this is a different thing entirely? Because I discover a creature of genius and try to help her to the position she deserves——"

"You hypocrite, if it had been a man instead of a charming little woman with big eyes, don't you know——"

But there had been a ring at the outer door, and Benson came in to say that a clergyman was waiting downstairs.

"Little Golightly again!" said Lord Robert wearily. "Are these everlasting arrangements never——"

The man stopped him. It was not Mr. Golightly; it was a stranger; would not give his name; looked like a Catholic priest; had been there before, he thought.

"Can it be—-Talk of the devil——"

"Ask him up," said Drake. And while Drake bit his lip and clinched his hands, and Lord Robert took up a scent bottle and sprayed himself with eau de cologne, they saw a man clad in the long coat of a priest come into the room—calm, grave, self-possessed, very pale, with hollow and shaven cheeks and dark and sunken eyes, which burned with a sombre fire, and head so closely cropped as to seem to be almost bald.

John Storm's anger had cooled. As he crossed the park the heat of his soul had turned to fear, and while he stood in the hall below, with an atmosphere of perfume about him, and even a delicate sense of a feminine presence, his fear had turned to terror. On that account he had refused to send up his name, and on going up the staircase, lined with prints, he had been tempted to turn about and fly lest he should come upon Glory face to face. But finding only the two men in the room above, his courage came back and he hated himself for his treacherous thought of her.

"You will forgive me for this unceremonious visit, sir," he said, addressing himself to Drake.

Drake motioned to him to be seated. He bowed, but continued to stand.

"Your friend will remember that I have been here before."

Lord Robert bent his head, and went on trifling with the spray.

"It was a painful errand relating to a girl who had been nurse at the hospital. The girl was nothing to me, but she had a companion who was very much."

Drake nodded and his lips stiffened, but he did not speak.

"You are aware that since then I have been away from the hospital. I wrote to you on the subject; you will remember that."

"Well?" said Drake.

"I have only just returned, and have come direct from the hospital now."

"Well?"

"I see you know what I mean, sir. My young friend has gone. Can you tell me where to find her?"

"Sorry I can not," said Drake coldly, and it stung him to see a look of boundless relief cross the grave face in front of him.

"Then you don't know——"

"I didn't say that," said Drake, and then the lines of pain came back.

"At the request of her people I brought her up to London. Naturally they will look to me for news of her, and I feel responsible for her welfare."

"If that is so, you must pardon me for saying you've taken your duty lightly," said Drake.

John Storm gripped the rail of the chair in front of him, and there was silence for a moment.

"Whatever I may have to blame myself with in the past, it would relieve me to find her well and happy and safe from all harm."

"She *is* well and happy, and safe too—I can tell you that much."

There was another moment of silence, and then John Storm said in broken sentences and in a voice that was struggling to control itself: "I have known her since she was a child, sir—-You can not think how many tender memories—-It is nearly a year since I saw her, and one likes to see old friends after an absence."

Drake did not speak, but he dropped his head, for John's eyes had begun to fill.

"We were good friends too. Boy and girl comrades almost. Brother and sister, I should say, for that was how I liked to think of myself—her elder brother bound to take care of her."

There was a little trill of derisive laughter from the other side of the room, where Lord Robert had put the spray down noisily and turned to look out into the street. Then John Storm drew himself up and said in a firm voice:

"Gentlemen, why should I mince matters? I will not do so. The girl we speak of is more to me than anybody else in the world besides. Perhaps she was one of the reasons why I went into that monastery. Certainly she is the reason I have come out of it. I have come to find her. I *shall* find her. If she is in difficulty or danger I intend to save her. Will you tell me where she is?"

"Mr. Storm," said Drake, "I am sorry, very sorry, but what you say compels me to speak plainly. The lady is well and safe and happy. If her friends are anxious about her she can reassure them for herself, and no doubt she has already done so. But in the position she occupies at present you are a dangerous man. It might not be her wish, and it would not be to her advantage, to meet with you, and I can, not allow her to run the risk."

"Has it come to that? Have you a right to speak for her, sir?"

"Perhaps I have——" Drake hesitated, and then said with a rush, "the right to protect her against a fanatic."

John Storm curbed himself; he had been through a long schooling. "Man, be honest," he said. "Either your interest is good or bad, selfish or unselfish. Which is it?"

Drake made no answer.

"But it would be useless to bandy words. I didn't come here to do that. Will you tell me where she is?"

"No."

"Then it is to be a duel between us—is that so? You for the girl's body and I for her soul? Very well, I take your challenge."

There was silence once more, and John Storm's eyes wandered about the room. They fixed themselves at length on the sketch by the pier-glass.

"On my former visit I met with the same reception. The girl could take care of herself. It was no business of mine. How that relation has ended I do not ask. But this one— —"

"This one is an entirely different matter," said Drake, "and I will thank you not to— —"

But John Storm was making the sign of the cross on his breast, and saying, as one who was uttering a prayer, "God grant it is and always may be!"

At the next moment he was gone from the room. The two men stood where he had left them until his footsteps had ceased on the stairs and the door had closed behind him. Then Drake cried, "Benson—a telegraph form! I must telegraph to Koenig at once."

"Yes, he'll follow her up on the double quick," said Lord Robert. "But what matter? His face will be enough to frighten the girl. Ugh! It was the face of a death's head!"

At dinner that night John Storm was more than usually silent. To break in upon his gravity, Mrs. Callender asked him what he intended to do next.

"To take priest's orders without delay," he said.

"And what then?"

"Then," he said, lifting a twitching and suffering face "to make an attack on the one mighty stronghold of the devil's kingdom whereof woman is the direct and immediate victim; to tell Society over again it is an organized hypocrisy for the pursuit and demoralization of woman, and the Church that bachelorhood is not celibacy, and polygamy is against the laws of God; to look and search for the beaten and broken who lie scattered and astray in our bewildered cities, and to protect them and shelter them whatever they are, however low they have fallen, because they are my sisters and I love them."

"God bless ye, laddie! That's spoken like a man," said the old woman, rising from her seat.

But John Storm's pale face had already flushed up to the eyes, and he dropped his head as one who was ashamed.

CHAPTER II

At eight o'clock that night John Storm was walking through the streets of Soho. The bell of a jam factory had just been rung, and a stream of young girls in big hats with gorgeous flowers and sweeping feathers were pouring out of an archway and going arm-in-arm down the pavement. Men standing in groups at street ends shouted to them as they passed, and they shouted back in shrill voices and laughed with wild joy. In an alley round one corner an organ man was playing "Ta-ra-ra-boom-de-ay," and some of the girls began to dance and sing around him. Coming to the main artery of traffic, they were almost run down by a splendid equipage which was cutting across two thoroughfares into a square, and they screamed with mock terror as the fat coachman in tippet and cockade bellowed to them to get out of the way.

The square was a centre of gaiety. Theatres and music halls lined two of its sides, and the gas on their facades and the beacons on their roofs were beginning to burn brightly in the fading daylight. With skips and leaps the girls passed over to the doors of these palaces, and peered with greedy eyes through lines of policemen and doorkeepers in livery at gentlemen, in shields of shirt-front and ladies in light cloaks and long white gloves stepping out of gorgeous carriages into gorgeous halls.

John Storm was looking on at this masquerade when suddenly he became aware that the flare of coarse lights on the front of the building before him formed the letters of a word. The word was "GLORIA." Seeing it again as he had seen it in the morning, but now identified and explained, he grew hot and cold by turns, and his brain, which refused to think, felt like a sail that is flapping idly on the edge of the wind.

There was a garden in the middle of the square, and he walked round and round it. He gazed vacantly at a statue in the middle of the garden, and then walked round the rails again. The darkness was gathering fast, the gas was beginning to blaze, and he was like a creature in the coil of a horrible fascination. That word, that name over the music hall, fizzing and crackling in its hundred lights, seemed to hold him as by an eye of fire. And remembering what had happened since he left the monastery—the sandwich men, the boards on the omnibuses, the hoardings on the walls—it seemed like a fiery finger which had led him to that spot. Only one thing was clear—that a supernatural power had brought him there, and that it was intended he should come. Fearfully, shamefully, miserably, rebuking himself for his doubts, yet conquered and compelled by them, he crossed the street and entered the music hall.

He was in the pit and it was crowded; not a seat vacant anywhere, and many persons standing packed in the crush-room at the back. His first sensation was of being stared at. First the man at the pay-box and then the check-taker had looked at him, and now he was being looked at by the people about him. They were both men and girls. Some of the men wore light frock-coats and talked in the slang of the race-course, some of the girls wore noticeable hats and showy flowers in their bosoms and were laughing in loud voices. They made a way for him of themselves, and he passed through to a wooden barrier that ran round the last of the pit seats.

The music hall was large, and to John Storm's eyes, straight from the poverty of his cell, it seemed garish in the red and gold of its Eastern decorations. Men in the pit seats were smoking pipes and cigarettes, and waiters with trays were hurrying up and down the aisles serving ale and porter, which they set down on ledges like the book-rests in church. In the stalls in front, which were not so full, gentlemen in evening dress were smoking cigars, and there was an arc of the tier above, in which people in fashionable costumes were talking audibly. Higher yet, and unseen from that position, there was a larger audience still, whose voices rumbled like a distant sea. A cloud of smoke filled the atmosphere, and from time to time there was the sound of popping corks and breaking glasses and rolling bottles.

The curtain was down, but the orchestra was beginning to play. Two men in livery came from the sides of the curtain and fixed up large figures in picture frames that were attached to the wings of the proscenium. Then the curtain rose and the entertainment was resumed. It was in sections, and after each performance the curtain was dropped and the waiters went round with their trays again.

John Storm had seen it all before in the days when, under his father's guidance, he had seen everything—the juggler, the acrobat, the step-dancer, the comic singer, the tableaus, and the living picture. He felt tired and ashamed, yet, he could not bring himself to go away. As the evening advanced he thought: "How foolish! What madness it was to think of such a thing!" He was easier after that, and began to listen to the talk of the people about him. It was free, but not offensive. In the frequent intervals some of the men played with the girls, pushing and nudging and joking with them, and the girls laughed and answered back. Occasionally one of them would turn her head aside and look into John's face with a saucy smile. "God forbid that I should grudge them their pleasure!" he thought. "It's all they have, poor creatures!"

But the audience grew noisier as the evening went on. They called to the singers, made inarticulate squeals, and then laughed at their own humour. A lady sang a comic song. It described her attempt to climb to the top of an omnibus on a windy day. John turned to look at the faces behind him, and every face was red and hot, and grinning and grimacing. He was still half buried in the monastery he had left that morning, and he thought: "Such are the nightly pleasures of our people. To-night, to-morrow night, the night after! O my country, my country!"

He was awakened from these thoughts by an outburst of applause. The curtain was down and nothing was going on except the putting up of a new figure in the frames. The figure was 8. Some one behind him said, "That's her number!" "The new artiste?" said another voice. "Gloria," said the first.

John Storm's head began to swim. He looked back—he was in a solid block of people. "After all, what reasons have I?" he thought, and he determined to stand his ground.

More applause. Another leader of the orchestra had appeared. *Bâton* in hand, he was bowing from his place before the footlights. It was Koenig, the organist, and John Storm shuddered in the darkest corner of his soul.

The stalls had filled up unawares to him, and a party was now coming into a private box which had hitherto been empty. The late-comers were Drake and Lord Robert Ure, and a lady with short hair brushed back from her forehead.

John Storm felt the place going round him, yet he steadied and braced himself. "But this is the natural atmosphere of such people," he thought. He tried to find satisfaction in the thought that Glory was not with them. Perhaps they had exaggerated their intimacy with her.

The band began to play. It was music for the entrance of a new performer. The audience became quiet; there was a keen, eager, expectant air; and then the curtain went up. John Storm felt dizzy. If he could have escaped he would have turned and fled. He gripped with both hands the rail in front of him.

Then a woman came gliding on to the stage. She was a tall girl in a dark dress and long black gloves, with red hair, and a head like a rose. It was Glory! A cloud came over John Storm's eyes, and for a few moments he saw no more.

There was some applause from the pit and the regions overhead. The people in the stalls were waving their handkerchiefs, and the lady in the box was kissing her hand. Glory was smiling, quite at her ease, apparently not at all nervous, only a little shy and with her hands interlaced in front of her. Then there was silence again and she began to sing.

It is the moment when prayers go up from the heart not used to pray. Strange contradiction! John Storm found himself praying that Glory might do well, that she might succeed and eclipse everything! But he had turned his eyes away, and the sound of her voice was even more afflicting than the sight of her face. It was nearly a year since he had heard it last, and now he was hearing it under these conditions, in a place like this! He must have been making noises by his breathing. "Hush! hush!" said the people about him, and somebody tapped him on the shoulder.

After a moment he regained control of himself, and he lifted his head and listened. Glory's voice, which had been quavering at first, gathered strength. She was singing Mylecharaine, and the wild, plaintive harmony of the old Manx ballad was floating in the air like the sound of the sea. After her first lines a murmur of approval went round, the people sat up and leaned forward, and then there was silence again—dead silence—and then loud applause.

But it was only with the second verse that the humour of her song began, and John Storm waited for it with a trembling heart. He had heard her sing it a hundred times in the old days, and she was singing it now as she had sung it before. There were the same tricks of voice, the same tricks of gesture, the same expressions, the same grimaces. Everything was the same, and yet everything was changed. He knew it. He was sure it must be so. So artless and innocent then, now so subtle and significant! Where was the difference? The difference was in the place, in the people. John Storm could have found it in his heart to turn on the audience and insult them. Foul-minded creatures, laughing, screaming, squealing, punctuating their own base interpretations and making evil of what was harmless! How he hated the grinning faces round about him!

When the song was finished Glory swept a gay courtesy, lifted her skirts, and tripped off the stage. Then there were shouting, whistling, stamping, and deafening applause. The whole house was unanimous for an encore, and she came back smiling and bowing with a certain look of elation and pride. John Storm was becoming terrified by his own anger. "Be quiet there!" said some one behind him. "Who's the josser?" said somebody else, and then he heard Glory's voice again.

It was another Manx ditty. A crew of young fishermen are going ashore on Saturday night after their week on the sea after the herring. They go up to the inn; their sweethearts meet them there; they drink and sing. At length they are so overcome by liquor and love that they have to be put to bed in their big sea boots. Then the girls kiss them and leave them. The singer imitated the kissing, and the delighted audience repeated the sound. Sounds of kissing came from all parts of the hall, mingled with loud acclamations of laughter. The singer smiled and kissed back. Somehow she conveyed the sense of a confidential feeling as if she were doing it for each separate person in the audience, and each person had an impulse to respond. It was irresistible, it was maddening, it swept over the whole house.

John Storm felt sick in his very soul. Glory knew well what she was doing. She knew what these people wanted. His Glory! Glory of the old, innocent happy days! O God! O God! If he could only get out! But that was impossible. Behind him the dense mass was denser than ever, and he was tightly wedged in by a wall of faces—hot, eager, with open mouths, teeth showing, and glittering and dancing eyes. He tried not to listen to what the people about were saying, yet he could not help but hear.

"Tasty, ain't she?" "Cerulean, eh?" "Bit 'ot, certinly!" "Well, if I was a Johnny, and had got the oof, she'd have a brougham and a sealskin to-morrow." "To-night, you mean," and then there were significant squeaks and trills of laughter.

They called her back again, and yet again, and she returned with unaffected cheerfulness and a certain look of triumph. At one moment she was doing the gaiety of youth, and at the next the crabbedness of age; now the undeveloped femininity of the young girl, then the volubility of the old woman. But John Storm was trying to hear none of it. With his head in his breast and his eyes down he was struggling to think of the monastery, and to imagine that he was still buried in his cell. It was only this morning that he left it, yet it seemed to be a hundred years ago. Last night the Brotherhood, the singing of Evensong, Compline, the pure air, silence, solitude, and the atmosphere of prayer; and to-night the crowds, the clouds of smoke, the odour of drink, the meaning laughter, and Glory as the centre of it all!

For a moment everything was blotted out, and then there was loud hand-clapping and cries of "Bravo!" He lifted his head. Glory had finished and was bowing herself off. The lady in the private box flung her a bouquet of damask roses. She picked it up and kissed it, and bowed to the box, and then the acclamations of applause were renewed.

The crush behind relaxed a little, and he began to elbow his way out. People were rising or stirring everywhere, and the house was emptying fast.

As the audience surged down the corridors to the doors they talked and laughed and made inarticulate sounds. "A tricky bit o' muslin, eh?" "Yus, she's thick." "She's my dart, anyhow." Then the whistling of a tune. It was the chorus of Mylecharaine. John Storm felt the cool air of the street on his hot face at last. The policemen were keeping a way for the people coming from the stalls, the doorkeepers were whistling or shouting for cabs, and their cries were being caught up by the match boys, who were running in and out like dogs among the carriage wheels and the horses' feet. "En-sim!" "Four-wheel-er!"

In a narrow court at the back, dimly lit and not much frequented, there was a small open door under a lamp suspended from a high blank wall. This was the stage-door of the music hall, and a group of young men, looking like hairdressers' assistants, blocked the pavement at either side of it. "Wonder what she's like off?" "Like a laidy, you bet." "Yus, but none o' yer bloomin' hamatoors." "Gawd, here's the josser again!"

John Storm pushed his way through to where a commissionaire sat behind a glass partition in a little room walled with pigeon holes.

"Can I see Miss Quayle?" he asked.

The porter looked blank.

"Gloria, then," said John Storm, with an effort.

The porter looked at him suspiciously. Had he an appointment? No; but could he send in his name? The porter looked doubtful. Would she come out soon? The porter did not know. Would she come this way? The porter could not tell. Could he have her address?

"If ye want to write to the laidy, write here," said the porter, with a motion of his hands to the pigeon-holes.

John Storm felt humiliated and ashamed. The hairdressers' assistants were grinning at him. He went out, feeling that Glory was farther than ever from him now, and if he met her they might not speak. But he could not drag himself away. In the darkness under a lamp at the other side of the street he stood and waited. Shoddy broughams drove up, with drivers in shabby livery, bringing "turns" in wonderful hats and overcoats, over impossible wigs, whiskers, and noses—niggers, acrobats, clowns, and comic singers, who stepped out, shook the straw of their carriage carpets off their legs, and passed in at the stage entrance.

At length the commissionaire appeared at the door and whistled, and a hansom cab rattled up to the end of the court. Then a lady muffled in a cape, with the hood drawn over her head, and carrying a bouquet of roses, came out leaning on the arm of a gentleman. She stood a moment by his side and spoke to him and laughed. John heard her laughter. At the next moment she had stepped into the hansom, the door had fallen to, the driver had turned, the gentleman had raised his hat, the light had fallen on the lady's face, and she was leaning forward and smiling. John saw her smiles.

At the next moment the hansom had passed into the illuminated thoroughfares and the group of people had dispersed. John Storm was alone under the lamp in the little dark street, and somewhere in the dark alleys behind him the organ man was still grinding out "Ta-ra-ra-boom-de-ay."

"Weel, what luck on your first night out?" said Mrs. Callender at breakfast in the morning. "Found any of the poor lost things yet?"

"One," said John, with a rueful face. "Lost enough, though she doesn't know it yet, God help her!"

"They never do at first, laddie. Write to her friends, if she has any."

"Her friends?"

"Nothing like home influences, ye ken."

"I will—I must! It's all I can do now."

CHAPTER III

"The Priory, Friday Morning.

"Oh, my dear aunties, don't be terrified, but Glory has had a kind of a wee big triumph! Nothing very awful, you know, but on Monday night, before a rather larger company than usual, she sang and recited and play-acted a little, and as a result all the earth—the London earth—is talking about her, and nobody is taking any notice of the rest of the world. Every post is bringing me flowers with ribbons and cards attached, or illustrated weeklies with my picture and my life in little, and I find it's wonderful what a lot of things you may learn about yourself if you'll only read the papers. My room at this moment is like a florist's window at nine o'clock on Saturday morning, and I have reason to suspect that mine host and teacher, Carl Koenig, F. E. C. O., exhibits them to admiring neighbours when I am out. The voice of that dear old turtle has ever since Monday been heard in the land, and besides telling me about Poland day and night from all the subterranean passages of the house, he has taken to waiting on me like a nigger, and ordering soups and jellies for me as if I had suddenly become an invalid. Of course, I am an able-bodied woman just the same as ever, but my nerves have been on the rack all the week, and I feel exactly as I did long ago at Peel when I was a little naughty minx and got up into the tower of the old church and began pulling at the bell rope, you remember. Oh, dear! oh, dear! My frantic terror at the noise of the big bells and the vibration of the shaky old walls! Once I had begun I couldn't leave off for my life, but went on tugging and tugging and quaking and quaking until—have you forgotten it?—all the people came running helter-skelter under the impression that the town was afire. And then, behold, it was only little me, trembling like a leaf and crying like a ninny! I remember I was scolded and smacked and dismissed into outer darkness (it was the chip vault, I think), for that first outbreak of fame, and now, lest you should want to mete out the same punishment to me again—

"Aunt Anna, I'm knitting the sweetest little shawl for you, dear—blue and white, to suit your complexion—being engaged in the evening only, and most of the day sole mistress of my own will and pleasure. How charming of me, isn't it? But I'm afraid it isn't, because you'll see through me like a colander, for I want to tell you something which I have kept back too long, and when I think of it I grow old and wrinkled like a Christmas apple. So you must be a pair of absolute old angels, aunties, and break the news to grandfather.

"You know I told you, Aunt Rachel, to say something for me at nine o'clock on the Queen's birthday. And you remember that Mr. Drake used to think pearls and diamonds of Glory, and predict wonderful things for her. Then you don't forget that Mr. Drake had a friend named Lord Robert Ure, commonly called Lord Bob. Well, you see, by Mr. Drake's advice, and Lord Bobbie's influence and agency, and I don't know what, I have made one more change—it's to be the last, dears, the very last—in my Wandering-Jew existence, and now I am no longer a society entertainer, because I am a music-hall art— —"

Glory had written so far when she dropped the pen and rose from the table, wiping her eyes.

"My poor child, you can't tell them, it's impossible; they would never forgive you!"

Then a carriage stopped before the house, the garden bell was rung, and the maid came into the room with a lady's card. It was inscribed "Miss Polly Love," with many splashes and flourishes.

"Ask her up," said Glory. And then Polly came rustling up the stairs in a silver-gray silk dress and a noticeable hat, and with a pug-dog tucked under her arm. She looked older and less beautiful. The pink and ivory of her cheeks was coated with powder, and her light gray eyes were pencilled. There was the same blemished appearance as before, and the crack in the vase was now plainly visible.

Glory had met the girl only once since they parted after the hospital, but Polly kissed her effusively. Then she sat down and began to cry.

"Perhaps you wouldn't think it, my dear, but I'm the most miserable girl in London. Haven't you heard about it? I thought everybody knew. Robert is going to be married. Yes, indeed, to-morrow morning to that American heiress, and I hadn't an idea of it until Monday afternoon. That was the day of your luncheon, dear, and I felt sure something was going to happen, because I broke my looking-glass dressing to go out. Robert took me home, and he began to play the piano, and I could see he was going to say something. 'Do you know, little woman, I'm to be married on Saturday?' I wonder I didn't drop, but I didn't, and he went on playing. But it was no use trying, and I burst out and ran into my room. After a minute I heard him coming in, but he didn't lift me up as he used to do. Only talked to me over my back, telling me to control myself, and what he was going to do for me, and so on. He used to say a few tears made me nicer looking, but it was no good crying—and then he went away."

She began to cry again, and the dog in her lap began to howl.

"O God! I don't know what I've done to be so unfortunate. I've not been flash at all, and I never went to *cafés* at night, or to Sally's or Kate's, as so many girls do, and he can't say I ever took notice of anybody else. When I love anybody I think of him last thing at night and first thing in the morning, and now to be left alone—I'm sure I shall never live through it!"

Glory tried to comfort the poor broken creature. It was her duty to live. There was her child—had she never even seen it since she parted with it to Mrs. Jupe? It must be such a darling by this time, creeping about and talking a little, wherever it was. She ought to have the child to live with her, it would be such company.

Polly kissed the pug to stop its whining, and said: "I don't want company. Life isn't the same thing to me now. He thinks because he is marrying that woman—What better is she than me, I would like to know? She's only snapping at him for what he is, and he is only taking her for what she's got, and I've a great mind to go to All Saints' and shame them. You wouldn't? Well, it's hard to hide one's feelings, but it would serve them right if—if I did it."

Polly had risen with a wild look, and was pressing the pug so hard that it was howling again.

"Did what?" said Glory.

"Nothing—that is to say——"

"You mustn't dream of going to the church. The police——"

"Oh, it isn't the police I'm afraid of," said Polly, tossing her head.

"What then?"

"Never mind, my dear," said Polly.

On the way downstairs she reproached herself for not seeing what was coming. "But girls like us never do, now do we?"

Glory coloured up to her hair, but made no protest. At the gate Polly wiped her eyes and drew down her veil, and said: "I'm sorry to say it to your face, my dear, but it's all been that Mr. Drake's doings, and a girl ought to know he'd do as much himself, and worse. But you're a great woman now, and in everybody's mouth, so you needn't care. Only——"

Glory's face was scarlet and her under lip was bleeding. Yet she kissed the poor shallow thing at parting, because she was down, and did not understand, and lived in another world entirely. But going back to where her letter lay unfinished she thought: "Impossible! If this girl, living in an atmosphere so different, thinks that——" Then she sat at the table and forced herself to tell all.

She had got through the red riot of her confession and was writing: "I don't know what he would think of it, but do you know I thought I saw his face on Wednesday night. It was in the dark, and I was in a cab driving away from the stage door. But so changed! oh, so changed! It must have been a dream, and it was the same as if his ghost had passed me."

Then she became aware of voices in dispute downstairs. First a man's voice, then the voices of two men—one of them Koenig's, the other with a haunting ring in it. She got up from the table and went to the door of her room, going on tip-toe, yet hardly knowing why. Koenig was saying: "No, sair, de lady does not lif here." Then a deep, strong chest-voice answered, "Mr. Koenig, surely you remember me?" and Glory's heart seemed to beat like a watch. "No-o, sair. Are you—Oh, yes; what am I thinking of?—But de lady——"

"Mr. Koenig," Glory called, cried, gasped over the stair-rail, "ask the gentleman to come up, please."

She hardly knew what happened next, only that Koenig seemed to be muttering confused explanations below, and that she was back in her sitting-room giving a glance into the looking-glass and doing something with her hair. Then there was a step on the stairs, on the landing, at the threshold, and she fell back a few paces from the door, that she might see him as he came in. He knocked. Her heart was beating so violently that she had to keep her hand over it. "Who's there?"

"It is I."

"Who's I?"

Then she saw him coming down on her, and the very sunlight seemed to wave like the shadows on a ship. He was paler and thinner, his great eyes looked weary though they smiled, his hand felt bony though firm, and his head was closely cropped.

She looked at him for a moment without speaking and with a sensation of fulness at her heart that was almost choking her.

"Is it you? I didn't know it was you—I was just thinking——" She was talking at random, and was out of breath as if she had been running.

"Glory, I have frightened you!"

"Frightened? Oh, no! Why should you think so? Perhaps I am crying, but then I'm always doing that nowadays. And, besides, you are so— —"

"Yes, I am altered," he said in the pause that followed.

"And I?"

"You are altered too." He was looking at her with an earnest and passionate gaze. It was she—herself—Glory—not merely a vision or a dream. Again he recognised the glorious eyes with their brilliant lashes and the flashing spot in one of them that had so often set his heart beating. She looked back at him and thought, "How ill he must have been!" and then a lump came into her throat and she began to laugh that she might not have to cry, and broke out into broad Manx lest he should hear the tremor in her voice:

"But you're coming too, aren't ye? And you've left that theer—Aw, it's glad ter'ble I am, as our people say, and it's longin' mortal you'd be for all, boy."

Another trill of nervous laughter, and then a burst of earnest English: "But tell me, you've come for good—you are not going back to— —"

"No, I am not going back to the Brotherhood, Glory." How friendly his low voice sounded!

"And you?"

"Well, I've left the hospital, you see."

"Yes, I see," he said. His weary eyes were wandering about the room, and for the first time she felt ashamed of its luxuries and its flowers.

"But how did you find me?"

"I went to the hospital first— —"

"So you hadn't forgotten me? Do you know I thought you had quite— But tell me at once, where did you go then?"

He was silent for a moment, and she said, "Well?"

"Then I went to Mr. Drake's chambers."

"I don't know why everybody should think that Mr. Drake— —"

His great eyes were fixed on her face and his mouth was quivering, and, to prevent him from speaking, she put on a look of forced gaiety and said, "But how did you light on me at last?"

"I meant to find you, Glory, if I tramped all London over and everybody denied you to me"—the lump in her throat was hurting her dreadfully—"but I chanced to see the name over the music hall."

She saw it coming, and broke into laughter. "The music hall! Only think! You looking at music halls!"

"I was there on Monday night."

"You? Monday? Then perhaps it was not my fancy that I saw you by the stage do—." Her nerves were getting more and more excited, and to calm them she crossed her arms above her head. "So they gave you my address at the stage door, did they?"

"No, I wrote for it to Peel."

"Peel?" She caught her breath, and her arms came down. "Then perhaps you told them where——" "I told them nothing, Glory." She looked at him through her eyelashes, her head held down.

"Not that it matters, you know."

"I've just been writing to them, and they'll soon—But, oh, I've so much to say, and I can't say it here. Couldn't we go somewhere? Into the park or on to the heath, or farther—much farther—the room is so small, and I feel as if I've been suffocating for want of air."

"I've something to say too, and if——"

"Then let it be to-morrow morning, and we'll start early, and you'll bring me back in time for the theatre. Say Paddington Station, at eleven—will that do?"

"Yes."

She saw him to the gate, and when he was going she wanted him to kiss her hand, so she pretended to do the high handshake, but he only held it for a moment and looked steadily into her eyes. The sunshine was pouring into the garden, and she was bareheaded. Her hair was coiled up, and she was wearing a light morning blouse. He thought she had never looked so beautiful. On getting into the omnibus at the end of the street he took a letter out of his vest pocket, and, being alone, he first carried it to his lips, then reopened and read it:

"See her at once, dear John, and keep in touch with her, and I shall be happy and relieved. As for your father, that old Chaise is going crazy and is sending Lord Storm crazy too. He has actually discovered that the dust the witch walks on who has cast the evil eye on you lies in front of Glenfaba gate, and he has been sweeping it up o' nights and scattering it in front of

Knockaloe! What simplicity! There are only two women here. Does the silly old gawk mean Rachel? or is it, perhaps, Aunt Anna?"

And while the omnibus joggled down the street, and the pale young clergyman with the great weary eyes was poring over his letter, Glory was sitting at her table and writing with flying fingers and a look of enthusiastic ecstasy:

"I've had three bites at this cherry. But who do you think has just been here? John!—John Storm! But then you know that he is back, and it wasn't merely my fancy that I saw him by the stage door. It seems as if people have been denying me to him, and he has been waiting for me and watching over me." (Blot.) "His voice is so low, but I suppose that comes to people who are much alone, and he is so thin and so pale, and his eyes are so large, and they have that deep look that cuts into the heart. He knew he was changed, and I think he was ashamed" (blot), "but of course I didn't let whit that I was taking notice, and I'm so happy for his sake, poor fellow! that he has escaped from his cage in that Salvation zoo that I know I shall make them split their sides in the theatre to-night." (Blot, blot.) "How tiresome! This ink must have got water in it somehow, and then my handwriting is such a hop-skip-and-a-jump anyway. But hoots!

"Why shouldn't I love Johnny,

"And why shouldn't Johnny love me?

"Glory."

CHAPTER IV

It was a beautiful May morning, and standing by the Paddington Station with the dog at his feet, he felt her approach instinctively as she came toward him with her free step in her white cambric dress under the light parasol fringed with lace. Her face was glowing with the fresh air, and she looked happy and bright. As they walked into the station she poured out a stream of questions about the dog, took possession of him straightway, and concluded to call him Don.

They agreed to spend the day at Burnham Beeches, and while he went for the tickets she stepped on to the platform. It was Saturday, the bookstall was ablaze with the picture papers, and one of them was prominently displayed at a page containing her own portrait. She wanted John to see this, so she invented an excuse for bringing him face to face with it, and then she laughed and he bought the paper.

The clerk recognised her—they could see that by the smile he kept in reserve—and a group of officers in the Guards, in flannels and straw hats, going down to their club at Maidenhead, looked at her and nudged each other as if they knew who she was. Her eyes danced, her lips smiled, and she was proud that John should see the first fruits of her fame. She was proud of him, too, with his bold walk and strong carriage, as they passed the officers in their negligent dress, with their red and blue neckties. But John's heart was aching, and he was wondering how he was to begin on the duty he had to do.

From the moment they started she gave herself up to the delights of their holiday, and even the groaning and cranking and joggling of the train amused her. When the Guards had got into their first-class carriage they had glanced at the open window where her brilliant eyes and rosy lips were gleaming behind a veil. John gazed at her with his slow and tender looks, and felt guilty and ashamed.

They left the train at Slough, and a wave of freshness, with an odour of verdure and sap, blew into their faces. The dog leaped and barked, and Glory skipped along with it, breaking every moment into enthusiastic exclamations. There was hardly any wind, and the clouds, which were very high overhead, were scarcely moving. It was a glorious day, and Glory's face wore an expression of perfect happiness.

They lunched at the old hotel in the town, with the window open, and the swallows darting in the air outside, and Glory, who took milk "for remembrance," rose and said, "I looks toward Mr. Storm," and then drank his health and swept him the prettiest courtesy. All through lunch she kept feeding the dog from her own fingers, and at the end rebuked him for spreading his bones in a half circle across the carpet, a thing which was never done, she said, in the best society, this side the Cannibal Islands.

"By-and-bye," he thought, "time enough by-and-bye," for the charm of her joy was infectious.

The sun was high when they started on their walk, and her face looked flushed and warm. But through the park-like district to the wood she raced with Don, and made him leap over her sunshade and roll over and over on the bright green grass. The larks were trilling overhead, everything was humming and singing.

"Let her have one happy day," he thought, and they began to call and shout to each other.

Then they came to the beeches, and, being sheltered from the fiery rays of the sun, she put down her sunshade and John took off his hat. The silence and gloom, the great gnarled trees, with their thews and sinews, their arms and thighs and loins, the gentle rustle of the breeze in the branches overhead, the deep accumulation of dead leaves underfoot, the fluttering of wings, the low cooing of pigeons, and all the mystery and wonder of the wood, brought a sense of awe, as on entering a mighty minster in the dusk. But this wore away presently, and Glory began to sing. Her pure voice echoed in the fragrant air, and the happiness so long pent up and starved seemed to bubble in every word and note.

"Isn't this better than singing in music halls?" he thought, and then he began to sing too, just like any happy boy, without thinking of yesterday or to-morrow, of before or after. She smiled at him. He smiled back. It was like a dream. After his long seclusion it was difficult to believe it could be true. The open air, the perfume of the leaves they were wading through, the silver bark of the birches and the blue peeps of the sky between, and then Glory walking with her graceful motion, and laughing and singing by his side! "I shall wake up in a minute," he thought, "I'm sure I shall!"

They sang one song together. It was Lasses and Lads, and to make themselves think it was the old time back again they took each other's hands and swung them to the tune. He felt her clasp like milk coursing through his body, and a great wave of tenderness swept up his hard resolve as sea-wrack is thrown up after a storm. "She is here; we are together; why trouble about anything more?" and the time flew by.

But their voices went wrong immediately, and they were soon in difficulties. Then she laughed, and they began again; but they could not keep together, and as often as they tried they failed. "Ah, it's not like the old days!" he thought, and a mood of sadness came over him. He had begun to observe in Glory the trace of the life she had passed through—words, phrases, ideas, snatches of slang, touches of moods which had the note of a slight vulgarity. When the dog took a bone uninvited she cried: "It's a click; you've sneaked it"; when John broke down in the singing she told him to "chuck it off the chest"; and when he stopped altogether she called him glum, and said she would "do it on her own."

"Why does he look so sorrowful?" she thought, and telling herself that this came to people who were much alone, she rattled on more recklessly than before.

She talked of the life of the music hall, the life at "the back," glorifying it by a tone of apology. It was all hurry-scurry, slap, dash, and drive; no time to consider effects; a succession of last acts and first nights; so it was really harder to be a music-hall woman than a regular actress. And the music-hall woman was no worse than other women—considering. Had he seen their ballet? It was fetching. Such pages! Simply darlings! *They* were the proud young birds of paradise whom toffs like those Guards came to see, and it was fun to see them pluming and preening themselves at the back, each for the eyes of her own particular lord in the stalls. Thus she flung out unfamiliar notes, hardly knowing their purport, but to John they were as slimy creatures out of the social mire she had struggled through. O London! London! Its shadow was over them even there, and go where they would, they could never escape from it.

His former thought began to hang about him again, and he asked her to tell him what had happened to her during his absence.

"Shall I?" she said. "Well, I brought three golden sovereigns out of the hospital to distribute among the people of London, but, bless you, they went nowhere."

"And what then?"

"Then—then Hope was a good breakfast but a bad supper, you know. But shall I tell you all? Yes, yes, I will."

She told him of Mrs. Jupe, and of the deception she had practised upon her people, and he turned his head that he might not see her tears. She told him of the "Three Graces," and of the stage manager—she called him the "stage damager"—and then *she* turned her head that she might hide her shame. She told him of Josephs, the bogus agent, and his face grew hard and his brown eyes looked black.

"And where did you say his place was?" he asked in a voice that vibrated and broke.

"I didn't say," she answered with a laugh and a tear.

She told him of Aggie, and of the foreign clubs, and of Koenig, and of the dinner party at the Home Secretary's, and then she skipped a step and cried:

> "*Ding, dong, dended,*
>
> *My tale's ended.*"

"And was it there you met Mr. Drake again?"

She replied with a nod.

"Never having seen him in the meantime?"

She pursed her lips and shook her head. "That's all over now, and what matter? I likes to be jolly and I allwis is!"

"But is it all over?" he said, and he looked at her again with the deep look that had cut into her heart.

"He's going to say something," she thought, and she began to laugh, but with a faint tremor, and giving the dog her parasol to carry in his mouth, she took off her hat, swung it in her hand by the brim, and set off to run.

There was the light shimmer of a pool at a level below, where the water had drained to a bottom and was inclosed by beeches. The trees seemed to hang over it with outstretched wings, like birds about to alight, and round its banks there were plots of violets which filled the air with their fragrance. It was a God-blest bit of ground, and when he came up with her she was standing at the edge of the marshy mere panting and on the point of tears, and saying, in a whisper, "Oh, how beautiful!"

"But however am I to get across?" she cried, looking with mock terror on the two inches of water that barely covered the grass, and at the pretty red shoes that peeped from under her dress.

Then something extraordinary occurred. She hardly knew what was happening until it was over. Without a word, without a smile, he lifted her up in his arms and carried her to the other side. She felt helpless like a child, as if suddenly she belonged to herself no longer. Her head had fallen on his shoulder and her heart was beating against his breast. Or was it *his* heart that was beating? When he put her down she was afraid she was going to cry, so she began to laugh and to say they mustn't lose that 7.30 to London or the "rag" would be rolling up without her and the "stage damager" would be using "cuss words."

They had to pass the old church of Stoke Pogis on the way back to the town, and after looking at its timber belfry and steeple John suggested that they should see the inside. The sexton was found working in the garden at the side of the house, and he went indoors for the keys. "Here they be, sir, and you being a pa'son I'll bide in the orchet. You and your young missus can look at the church without me. 'A b'lieve 'a hev seed it afore," he said with a twinkle.

The church was dark and cool. There was a window representing an angel ascending to heaven against a deep blue sky, and a squire's pew furnished like a box at the theatre, with a carpet and even a stove. The chairs in the front bore family crests, and behind them were inferior chairs, without crests, for the servants. John had opened the little modern organ and begun to play. After a while he began to sing. He sang Nazareth, and his voice filled the empty church and went up into the gloom of the roof, and echoed and returned, and it was almost as if another voice were singing there.

Glory stood by his side and listened; a wonderful peace had come down on her. Then the emotion that vibrated in his deep voice made something surge up to her throat. "Life for evermore! Life for evermore!" All at once she began to weep, to sob, and to laugh in a breath, and he stopped.

"How ridiculous I am to-day! You'll think me a maniac," she said. But he only took her hand as if she had been a child and led her out of the church.

Insensibly the day had passed into evening, and the horizontal rays of the sun were dazzling their eyes as they returned to the hotel for tea. In giving orders for this meal they had left the illustrated weekly behind, and it was now clear from the easy smiles that greeted them that the paper had been looked at and Glory identified. The room was ready, with the table laid, the window closed, and a fire of wood in the dog grate, for the chill of the evening was beginning to be felt. And to make him forget what had happened at the church she put on a look of forced gaiety and talked rapidly, frivolously, and at random. The fresh air had given her such a colour that they would 'fairly eat her to-night.' How tired she was, though! But a cup of tea would exhilarate her "like a Johnnie's first whisky and soda in bed."

He looked at her with his grave face; every word was cutting him like a knife. "So you didn't tell the old folks at Glenfaba about the hospital until later?"

"No. Have a cup of the 'girl'? They call champagne 'the boy' at 'the back,' so I call tea 'the girl,' you know."

"And when did you tell them about the music hall?"

"Yesterday. 'Muffins?'" and as she held out the plate she waggled the wrist of her other hand, and mimicked the cry of the muffin man.

"Not until yesterday?"

She began to excuse herself. What was the use of taking people by surprise? And then good people were sometimes so easily shocked! Education and upbringing, and prejudices and even blood— —

"Glory," he said, "if you are ashamed of this life, believe me it is not a right one."

"Ashamed? Why should I be ashamed? Everybody is saying how proud I should be."

She spoke feverishly, and by a sudden impulse she plucked up the paper, but as suddenly let it drop again, for, looking at his grave face, her little fame seemed to shrivel up. "But give a dog a bad name you know— — You were there on Monday night. Did you see anything, now—anything in the performance— —"

"I saw the audience, Glory; that was enough for me. It is impossible for a girl to live long in an atmosphere like that and be a good woman. Yes, my child, impossible' God forbid that I should sit in judgment on any man, still less on any woman!—but the women of the music hall, do they remain good women? Poor souls, they are placed in a position so false that it would require extraordinary virtue not to become false along with it! And the whiter the soul that is dragged through that—that mire, the more the defilement. The audiences at such places don't want the white soul, they don't want the good woman, they want the woman who has tasted of the tree of good and evil. You can see it in their faces, and hear it in their laughter, and measure it in their applause. Oh, I'm only a priest, but I've seen these places all the world over, and I know what I'm saying, and I know it's true and you know it's true, Glory— —"

Glory leaped up from the table and her eyes seemed to emit fire. "I know it's hard and cruel and pitiless, and, since you were there on Monday and saw how kind the audience was to *me*, it's personal and untrue as well."

But her voice broke and she sat down again and said in another tone: "But, John, it's nearly a year, you know, since we saw each other last, and isn't it a pity? Tell me, where are you living now? Have you made your plans for the future? Oh, who do you think was with me just before you called yesterday? Polly—Polly Love, you remember! She's grown stout and plainer, poor thing, and I was so sorry——Her brother was in your Brotherhood, wasn't he? Is he as strangely fond of her as ever? Is he? Eh? Don't you understand? Polly's brother, I mean?"

"He's dead, Glory. Yes, dead. He died a month ago. Poor boy, he died broken-hearted! He had come to hear of his sister's trouble at the hospital. I was to blame for that. He never looked up again."

There was silence; both were gazing into the fire, and Glory's mouth was quivering. All at once she said: "John—John Storm, why can't you understand that it's not the same with me as with other women? There seem to be two women in me always. After I left the hospital I went through a good deal. Nobody will ever know how much I went through. But even at the worst, somehow I seemed to enjoy and rejoice in everything. Things happened that made me cry, but there was another me that was laughing. And that's how it is with the life I am living now. It is not I myself that go through this—this mire, as you call it, it's only my other self, my lower self, if you like, but I am not touched by it at all. Don't you see that? Don't you, now?"

"There are professions which are a source of temptation, and talents that are a snare, Glory——"

"I see, I see what you mean. There are not many ways a woman can succeed in—that's the cruelty of things. But there are a few, and I've chosen the one I'm fit for. And now, now that I've escaped from all that misery, that meanness, and have brought the eyes of London upon me, and the world is full of smiles for me, and sunshine, and I am happy, you come at last, you that I couldn't find when I wanted you so much—oh, so much!—because you had forgotten me; you come to me out of a darkness like the grave and tell me to give it all up. Yes, yes, yes, that's what you mean—give it all up! Oh, it's cruel!"

She covered her face with her hands and sobbed. He bent over her with a sorrowful face and said, "My child, if I have come out of a darkness as of the grave it is because I had *not* forgotten you there, but was thinking of you every day and hour."

Her sobbing ceased, but the tears still flowed through her fingers.

"Before that poor lad abandoned hope he came out into the world too-stole out-thinking to find his lost one. I told him to look for you first, and he went to the hospital."

"I saw him."

"You!"

"It was on New Year's Eve. He passed me in the street."

"Ah!—Well, he came back anyway, and said you were gone, and all trace of you was lost. Did I forget you after that, Glory?"

His husky voice broke off suddenly, and he rose with a look of wretchedness. "You are right, there are two selves in you, and the higher self is so pure, so strong, so unselfish, so noble—Oh, I am sure of it, Glory! Only there's no one to speak to it, no one. I try, but I can not."

She was still crying behind her hands.

"And meanwhile the lower self—there are only too many to speak to *that——*"

Her hands came down from her disordered face and she said, "I know whom you mean."

"I mean the world."

"No, indeed, you mean Mr. Drake. But you are mistaken. Mr. Drake has been a good friend to me, but he isn't anything else, and doesn't want to be. Can't you see that when you think of me and talk of me as you would of some other women you hurt me and degrade me, and I can not bear it? You see I am crying again—goodness knows why. But I sha'n't give up my profession. The idea of such a thing! It's ridiculous! Think of Glory in a convent! One of the poor Clares perhaps!"

"Hush!"

"Or back in the island serving out sewing at a mothers' meeting! Give it up! Indeed I won't!"

"You shall and you must!"

"Who'll make me?"

"*I* will!"

Then she laughed out wildly, but stopped on the instant and looked up at him with glistening eyes. An intense blush came over her face, and her looks grew bright as his grew fierce. A moment afterward the waiting maid, with an inquisitive expression, was clearing the table and keeping a smile in reserve for "the lovers' quarrel!"

Some of the Guardsmen were in the train going back, and at the next station they changed to the carriage in which Glory and John were sitting. Apparently they had dined before leaving their club at Maidenhead, and they talked at Glory with covert smiles. "Going to the Colosseum tonight?" said one. "If there's time," said another. "Oh, time enough. The attraction doesn't begin till ten, don't you know, and nobody goes before." "Tell me she's rippin'." "Good—deuced good."

Glory was sitting with her back to the engine drumming lightly on the window and looking out at the setting sun. At first she felt a certain shame at the obvious references, but, piqued at John's silence, she began to take pride in them, and shot glances at him from under half-closed eyelids. John was sitting opposite with his arms folded. At the talk of the men he felt his hands contract and his lips grow cold with the feeling that Glory belonged to everybody now and was common property. Once or twice he looked at them and became conscious of an impression, which had floated about him since he left the Brotherhood, that nearly every face he saw bore the hideous stamp of self-indulgence and sensuality.

But the noises of the train helped him not to hear, and he looked out for London. It lay before them under a canopy of smoke, and now and then a shaft from the setting sun lit up a glass roof and it glittered like a sinister eye. Then there came from afar, over the creaking and groaning of the wheels and the whistle of the engine, the deep, multitudinous murmur of that distant sea. The mighty tide was rising and coming up to meet them. Presently they were dashing into the midst of it, and everything was drowned in the splash and roar.

The Guardsmen, being on the platform side, alighted first, and on going off they bowed to Glory with rather more than easy manners. A dash of the devil prompted her to respond demonstratively, but John had risen and was taking off his hat to the men, and they were going away discomfited. Glory was proud of him—he was a man and a gentleman.

He put her into a hansom under the lamps outside the station, and her face was lit up, but she patted the dog and said: "You have vexed me and you needn't come to see me again. I shall not sing properly this evening or sleep tonight at all, if that is any satisfaction to you, so you needn't trouble to inquire."

When he reached home Mrs. Callender told him of a shocking occurrence at the fashionable wedding at All Saints' that morning. A young woman had committed suicide during the ceremony, and it turned out to be the poor girl who had been dismissed from the hospital.

John Storm remembered Brother Paul. "I must bury her," he thought.

CHAPTER V

Glory sang that night with extraordinary vivacity and charm and was called back again and again. Going home in the cab she tried to live through the day afresh—every step, every act, every word, down to that triumphant "*I* will." Her thoughts swayed as with the swaying of the hansom, but sometimes the thunderous applause of the audience broke in, and then she had to remember where she had left off. She could feel that beating against her breast still, and even smell the violets that grew by the pool. He had told her to give up everything, and there was an exquisite thrill in the thought that perhaps some day she would annihilate herself and all her ambitions, and—who knows what then?

This mood lasted until Monday morning, when she was sitting in her room, dressing very slowly and smiling at herself in the glass, when the Cockney maid came in with a newspaper which her master had sent up on account of its long report of the wedding.

"The Church of All Saints' was crowded by a fashionable congregation, among whom were many notable persons in the world of politics and society, including the father of the bridegroom, the Duke of — — and his brother, the Marquis of — —. An arch of palms crossed the nave at the entrance to the chancel, and festoons of rare flowers were suspended from the rails of the handsome screen. The altar and the table of the commandments were almost obscured by the wreaths of exotics that hung over them, and the columns of the colonnade, the font and offertory boxes were similarly buried in rich and lovely blossom.

"Thanks to an informal rehearsal some days before, the ceremony went off without a hitch. The officiating clergy were the Venerable Archdeacon Wealthy, D. D., assisted by the Rev. Josiah Golightly and other members of the numerous staff of All Saints'. The service, which was fully choral, was under the able direction of the well-known organist and choirmaster, Mr. Carl Koenig, F. R. C. O., and the choir consisted of twenty adult and forty boy voices. On the arrival of the bride a procession was formed at the west entrance and proceeded up to the chancel, singing 'The voice that breathed o'er Eden——"

"Poor Polly!" thought Glory.

"The bride wore a duchess satin gown trimmed with chiffon and Brussels lace, and having a long train hung from the shoulders. Her tulle veil was fastened with a ruby brooch and with sprays of orange blossom sent specially from the Riviera, and her necklace consisted of a rope of graduated pearls fully a yard long, and understood to have belonged to the jewel case of Catharine of Russia. She carried a bouquet of flowers (the gift of the bridegroom) brought from Florida, the American home of her family. The bride's mother wore — — The bridesmaids were dressed — —Mr. Horatio Drake acted as best man — —"

Glory drew her breath as with a spasm and threw down the newspaper. How blind she had been, how vain, how foolish! She had told John Storm that Drake was only a good friend to her, meaning him to understand that thus far she allowed him to go and no farther. But there was a whole realm of his life into which he did not ask her to enter. The "notable persons in politics and society," "the bridesmaids," these made up his real sphere, his serious scene. Other women were his friends, companions, equals, intimates, and when he stood in the eye of the world it was they who stood beside him. And she? She was his hobby. He came to her in his off hours. She filled up the under side of his life.

With a crushing sense of humiliation she was folding up the newspaper to send it downstairs when her eye was arrested by a paragraph in small type in the corner. It was headed "Shocking occurrence at a fashionable wedding."

"Oh, good gracious!" she cried. A glance had shown her what it was. It was a report of Polly's suicide.

"At a fashionable wedding at a West-End church on Saturday" (no names) "a young woman who had been sitting in the nave was seen to rise and attempt to step into the aisle, as if with the intention of crushing her way out, when she fell back in convulsions, and on being removed was found to be dead. Happily, the attention of the congregation was at the moment directed to the bride and bridegroom, who were returning from the vestry with the bridal party behind them, and thus the painful incident made no sensation among the crowded congregation. The body was removed to the parish mortuary, and from subsequent inquiries it transpired that death had been due to poison self-administered, and that the deceased was Elizabeth Anne Love (twenty-four), of no occupation, but formerly a nurse—a circumstance which had enabled her to procure half a grain of liquor strychninae on her own signature at a chemist's where she had been known."

"O God! O God!" Glory understood everything now. "I've a great mind to go to All Saints' and shame them—Oh, it isn't the police I'm afraid of." Polly's purpose was clear. She had intended to fall dead at the feet of the bride and bridegroom and make them walk over her body. Poor, foolish, ineffectual Polly! Her very ghost must be ashamed of the failure of her revenge. Not a ripple of sensation on Saturday, and this morning only a few obscure lines in little letters!

Oh, it was hideous! The poor thing's vengeance was theatrical and paltry, but what of the man, wherever he was? What did he think of himself now, with his millions and his murder? Yes, his murder, for what else was it?

An hour later Glory was ringing the bell of a little house in St. John's Wood whereof the upper blinds were drawn. The grating of the garden door slid back and an untidy head looked out.

"Well, ma'am?"

"Don't you remember me, Liza?"

"Lawd, yus, miss!" and the door was opened immediately; "but I was afeard you was one o' them reportin' people, and my orders is not to answer no questions.'"

"Has *he* been here, then?"

"Blesh ye, no, miss! He's on 'is way to the Continents. But 'is friend 'as, and he's settled everything 'andsome—I will say that for the gentleman."

Glory felt her gall rising; there was something degrading, almost disreputable, even in the loyalty of Drake's friendship.

"Fancy Liza not knowing you, miss, and me at the moosic 'all a Tuesday night! I 'ope you'll excuse the liberty, but I *did* laugh, and I won't say but I shed a few tears too. Arranged? Yes, the jury and the coroner and every-think. It's to be at twelve o'clock, so you may think I've 'ad my 'ands full. But you'll want to look at 'er, pore thing! Go up, miss, and mind yer 'ead; there's nobody but 'er friends with 'er now."

The friends proved to be Betty Belmont and her dressing-room companions. When Glory entered they showed no surprise. "The pore child told us all about you," said Betty; and the little one said: "It's your nyme that caught on, dear. The minute I heard it I said what a top-line for a, bill!"

It was the same little bandbox of a bedroom, only now it was darkened and Polly's troubles were over. There was a slightly convulsed look about the mouth, but the features were otherwise calm and childlike, for all the dead are innocent.

The three women with demure faces were sipping Benedictine and talking among themselves, and Polly's pug dog was coiled up on the bare bolster and snoring audibly.

"Pore thing! I don't know how she could 'a done it. But there, that's the worst of this life! It's all in the present and leads to nothing and ain't got no future." "What could the pore thing do? She wasn't so wonderful pretty; and then men like——" "She was str'ight with him, say what yer like. Only she ought to been more patienter, and she needn't 'a been so hard on the lady, neither." "She had everything the heart could wish. Look at her rooms! I wonder who'll——"

Carriages were heard outside, and two or three men came in to do the last offices. Glory had turned her face away, but behind her the women were still talking. "Wait a minute, mister! ... What a lovely ring! ... I wish I had a keepsake to remember her by." "Well, and why not? She won't want——"

Glory felt as if she was choking, but Polly's pug dog had been awakened by the commotion and was beginning to howl, so she took up the little mourner and carried it out. An organ-man somewhere near was playing Sweet Marie.

The funeral was at Kensal Green, and the four girls were the only followers. The coroner's verdict being *felo-de-se*, the body was not taken into the chapel, but a clergyman met it at the gate and led the way to the grave. Walking with her head down and the dog under her arm, Glory had not seen him at first, but when he began with the tremendous words, "I am the resurrection and the life," she caught her breath and looked up. It was John Storm.

While they were in the carriage the clouds had been gathering, and now some spots of rain were falling. When the bearers had laid down their burden the spots were large and frequent, and all save one of the men turned and went back to the shelter of the porch. The three women looked at each other, and one of them muttered something about "the dead and the living," and then the little lady stole away. After a moment the tall one followed her, and from shame of being ashamed the third one went off also.

By this time the rain was falling in a sharp shower, and John Storm, who was bareheaded, had opened his book and begun to read: "Forasmuch as it hath pleased Almighty God of his great mercy to take unto himself the soul of our dear sister here departed——"

Then he saw that Glory was alone by the graveside, and his voice faltered and almost failed him. It faltered again, and he halted when he came to the "sure and certain hope," but after a moment it quivered and filled out and seemed to say, "Which of us can sound the depths of God's design?" After the "maimed rites" were over, John Storm went back to the chapel to remove his surplice, and when he returned to the grave Glory was gone.

She sang as usual at the music hall that night, but with a heavy heart. The difference communicated itself to the audience, and the unanimous applause which had greeted her before frayed off at length into separate hand-claps. Crossing the stage to her dressing-room she met Koenig, who came to conduct for her, and he said:

"Not quite yourself to-night, my dear, eh?"

Going home in the hansom, Polly's dog coddled up with the old sympathy to the new mistress, and seemed to be making the best of things. The household was asleep, and Glory let herself in with a latch-key. Her cold supper was laid ready, and a letter was lying under the turned-down lamp. It was from her grandfather, and had been written after church on Sunday night:

"It is now so long—more than a year—since I saw my runaway and truant that, notwithstanding the protests of Aunt Anna and the forebodings of Aunt Rachel, I have determined to give my old legs a journey and my old eyes a treat. Therefore take warning that I intend to come up to London forthwith, that I may see the great city for the first time in my life, and— which is better—my little granddaughter among all her new friends and in the midst of her great prosperity."

At the foot of this there was a postscript from Aunt Rachel, hastily scrawled in pencil:

"Take no notice of this. He is far too weak to travel, and indeed he is really failing; but your letter, which reached us last night, has so troubled him ever since that he can't take rest for thinking of it."

It was the last straw. Before finishing the letter or taking off her hat, Glory took up a telegraph form and wrote, "Postpone journey—am returning home to-morrow." Then she heard Koenig letting himself into the house, and going downstairs she said:

"Will you take this message to the telegraph office for me, please?"

"Vhy, of course I vill, and den ve'll have supper togeder—look!" and he laughed and opened a paper and drew out a string of sausages.

"Mr. Koenig," she said, "you were right. I was not myself to-night. I want a rest, and I propose to take one."

As Glory returned upstairs she heard stammerings, sputterings, and swearings behind her about managers, engagements, announcements, geniuses, children, and other matters. Back in her room she lay down on the floor, with her face in her hands, and sobbed. Then Koenig appeared, panting and saying: "Dere! I knew vhat vould happen! Here's a pretty ting! And dat's vhy Mr. Drake told me to deny you to de man. De brute, de beast, de dirty son of a monk!"

But Glory had leaped up with eyes of fire, and was crying: "How dare you, sir? Out of my room this instant!"

"Mein Gott! It's a divil!" Koenig was muttering like a servant as he went downstairs. He went out to the telegraph office and came back, and then Glory heard him frying his sausages on the dining-room fire.

The night was far gone when she pushed aside her untouched supper, and, wiping her eyes, that she might see properly, sat down to write a letter.

"Dear John Storm (monk, monster, or whatever it is!): I trust it will be counted to me for righteousness that I am doing your bidding and giving up my profession—for the present.

> *"Between a woman's 'yes' and 'no'*
>
> *There isn't room for a pin to go,*

which is very foolish of her in this instance, considering that she is earning various pounds a night and has nothing but Providence to fall back upon. I have told my jailer I must have my liberty, and, being a man of like passions with yourself, he has been busy blaspheming in the parlour downstairs. I trust virtue will be its own reward, for I dare say it is all I shall ever get. If I were Narcissus I should fall in love with myself to-day, having shown an obedience to tyranny which is beautiful and worthy of the heroic age. But to-morrow morning I go back to the 'oilan,' and it will be so nice up there without anybody and all alone!"

She was laughing softly to herself as she wrote, and catching her breath with a little sob at intervals.

"A letter now and then is profitable to the soul of man—and—woman; but you must not expect to hear from *me*, and as for you, though you *have* resurrected yourself, I suppose a tyrant of your opinions will continue the Benedictine rule which compels you to hold your peace—and other things. I am engaged to breakfast with a nice girl named Glory Quayle to-morrow morning—that is to say, *this* morning—at Euston Station at a quarter to seven, but happily this letter won't reach you until 7.30, so I'll just escape interruption."

The house was still and the streets were quiet, not even a cab going along.

"Good-bye! I've realized—a dog! It's a pug, and therefore, like somebody else, it always looks black at me, though I suspect its father married beneath him, for it talks a good deal, and evidently hasn't been brought up in a Brotherhood. Therefore, being a 'female,' I intend to call it Aunt Anna—except when the original is about. Aunt Anna has been hopping up and down the room at my heels for the last hour, evidently thinking that a rational woman would behave better if she went to bed. Perhaps I shall take a leaf out of your book and 'comb her hair,' when I get her all alone in the train to-morrow, that she may be prepared for the new sphere to which it has pleased Providence to call her.

"Good-bye again! I see the lamps of Euston running after each other, only it's the *other* way this time. I find there is something that seizes you with a fiercer palpitation than coming *into* a great and wonderful city, and that is going out of one. Dear old London! After all, it has been very good to me. No one, it seems to me, loves it as much as I do. Only somebody thinks—well, never mind! Goodbye 'for all!' Glory."

At seven next morning, on the platform at Euston, Glory was standing with melancholy eyes at the door of a first-class compartment watching the people sauntering up and down, talking in groups and hurrying to and fro, when Drake stepped up to her. She did not ask what had brought him—she knew. He looked fresh and handsome, and was faultlessly dressed.

"You are doing quite right, my dear," he said in a cheerful voice. "Koenig telegraphed, and I came to see you off. Don't bother about the theatre; leave everything to me. Take a rest after your great excitement, and come back bright and well."

The locomotive whistled and began to pant, the smoke rose to the roof, the train started, and before Glory knew she was going she was gone.

Then Drake walked to his club and wrote this postscript to a letter to Lord Robert Ure, at the Grand Hotel, Paris: "The Parson has drawn first blood, and Gloria has gone home!"

CHAPTER VI

On the Sunday evening after Glory's departure John Storm, with the bloodhound running by his side, made his way to Soho in search of the mother of Brother Andrew. He had come to a corner of a street where the walls of an ugly brick church ran up a narrow court and turned into a still narrower lane at the back. The church had been for some time disused, and its facade was half covered with boardings and plastered with placards: "Brighton and Back, 3s."; "*Lloyd's News*"; "Coals, 1s. a cwt."; and "Barclay's Sparkling Ales."

There was a tumult in the court and lane. In the midst of a close-packed ring of excited people, chiefly foreigners, shouting in half the languages of Europe, a tall young Cockney, with bloated face and eyes aflame with drink, was writhing and wrestling and cursing. Sometimes he escaped from the grasp of the man who held him, and then he flung himself against the closed door of a shop which stood opposite, with the three balls of the pawnbroker suspended above it. Somebody within the shop was howling for help. It was a woman's voice, and the louder she screamed the more violent were the man's efforts to beat down the door between them.

As John Storm stood a moment looking on, some one on the street beside him said, "It's a d — — shyme." It was a man with a feeble, ineffectual face and the appearance of a waiter. Seeing he had been overheard, the man stammered: "Beg parding, sir; but they may well say 'when the Devil can't come hisself 'e sends 'is brother Drink.'" Having said this he began to move along, but stopped suddenly on seeing what the clergyman with the dog was doing.

John Storm was pushing his way through the crowd, and his black figure in that writhing ring of undersized foreigners looked big and commanding. "What's this?" he was saying in a husky voice that rose clear above the clamour. The shouting and swearing subsided, all save the howling from the inside of the shop, and the tumult settled down in a moment to mutterings and gnashings and a broken and irregular silence.

Then somebody said, "It's nothink, sir." And somebody else said, "'Es on'y drunk, and wantin' to pench 'is mother." Without listening to this explanation John Storm had laid hold of the young man by the collar and was dragging him, struggling and fuming, from the door.

"What's going on?" he demanded. "Will nobody speak?"

Then a poor swaggering imitation of a man came up out of the cellar of a house that stood next to the disused church, and a comely young woman carrying a baby followed close behind him. He had a gin bottle in his hands, and with a wink he said: "A christenin'—that's what's going on. 'Ave a kepple o' pen'orth of 'ollands, old gel?"

At this sally the crowd recovered its audacity and laughed, and the drunken man began to say that he could "knock spots out of any bloomin' parson, en' now bloomin' errer."

But the young fellow with the gin bottle broke in again. "What's yer gime, mister? Preach the gawspel? Give us trecks? This is my funeral, down't ye know, and I'd jest like to hear."

The little foreigners were enjoying the parson-baiting, and the drunken man's courage was rising to fever heat. "I'll give 'im one-two between the eyes if 'e touches me again." Then he flung himself on the pawnshop like a battering ram, the howling inside, which had subsided, burst out afresh, and finally the door was broken down.

Half a minute afterward the crowd was making a wavering dance about the two men. "Look out, ducky!" the young fellow shouted to John. The warning came too late—John went reeling backward from a blow.

"Now, my lads, who says next?" cried the drunken ruffian. But before the words were out of his mouth there was a growl, a plunge, a snarl, and he was full length on the street with the bloodhound's muzzle at his throat.

The crowd shrieked and began to fly. Only one person seemed to remain. It was an elderly woman, with dry and straggling gray hair. She had come out of the pawnshop and thrown herself on the dog in an effort to rescue the man underneath, crying: "My son—oh, my son! It'll kill him! Tyke the beast away!"

John Storm called the dog off, and the man got up unhurt, and nearly sober. But the woman continued to moan over the ruffian and to assail John and his dog with bitter insults. "We want no truck with parsons 'ere," she shouted.

"Stou thet, mother. It was my fault," said the sobered man, and then the woman began to cry. At the next minute John Storm was going with mother and son into the shut-up pawnshop, and the unhinged door was being propped behind them.

The crowd was trailing off when he came out again half an hour afterward, and the only commotion remaining was caused by a belated policeman asking, "Wot's bin the matter 'ere?" and by the young fellow with the gin bottle performing a step-dance on the pavement before the entrance to the cellar. The old woman stood at her door wiping her eyes on her apron, and her son was behind with a face that was now red from other causes than drink and rage.

"Good-bye, Mrs. Pincher; I may see you again soon."

Hearing this, the young swaggerer stopped his step-dancing and cried: "What cheer, myte? Was it a blowter and a cup of cawfy?"

"For shynie, Charlie!" cried the girl with a baby, and the young fellow answered, "Shut yer 'ead, Aggie!"

The waiter was still at the corner of the court, and when John came up he spoke again. "There must be sem amoosement knockin' women abart, but I can't see it myself." Then in a simple way he began to talk about his "missis," and what a good creature she was, and finally announced himself "gyme" to help a parson "as stood up to that there drunken blowke for sake of a woman."

"What's your name?" said John.

"Jupe," said the man, and then something stirred in John's memory.

On the following day John Storm dined with his uncle at Downing Street. The Prime Minister was waiting in the library. In evening dress, with his back to the fireplace and his hands enlaced behind him, he looked even more thin and gaunt than before. He welcomed John with a few familiar words and a smile. His smile was brief and difficult, like that which drags across the face of an invalid. Dinner was announced immediately, and the old man took the young one's arm and they passed into the dining-room.

The panelled chamber looked cold and cheerless. It was lighted by a single lamp in the middle of the table. They took their seats at opposite sides. The statesman's thin hair shone on his head like streaks of silver. John exercised a strong physical influence upon him, and all through the dinner his bleak face kept smiling.

"I ought to apologize for having nobody to meet you, but I had something to say—something to suggest—and I thought perhaps——"

John interrupted with affectionate protestations, and a tremor passed over the wrinkles about the old man's eyes.

"It is a great happiness to me, my dear boy, that you have turned your back on that Brotherhood, but I presume you intend to adhere to the Church?"

John intended to take priest's orders without delay, and then go on with his work as a clergyman.

"Just so, just so"—the long, tapering fingers drummed on the table—"and I should like to do something to help you."

Then sipping at his wine-glass of water, the Prime Minister, in his slow, deep voice and official tone, began to detail his scheme. There was a bishopric vacant. It was only a colonial one—the Bishopric of Colombo. The income was small, no more than seventeen hundred pounds, the work was not light, and there were fifty clergy. Then a colonial bishopric was not usually a stepping-stone to preferment at home, yet still——

John interrupted again. "You are most kind, uncle, but I am only looking forward to living the life of a poor priest, out of sight of the world and the Church."

"Surely Colombo is sufficiently out of sight, my boy?"

"But I see no necessity to leave London."

The Prime Minister glanced at him steadily, with the concentrated expression of a man who is accustomed to penetrate the thoughts and feelings of another.

"Why then—why did you——"

"Why did I leave the monastery, uncle? Because I had come to see that the monastic system was based on a faulty ideal of Christianity, which had been tried for the greater part of nineteen hundred years and failed. The theory of monasticism is that Christ died to redeem our carnal nature, and all we have to do is to believe and pray. But it is not enough that Christ died once. He must be dying always—every day—and in every one of us. God is calling on us in this age to seek a new social application of the Gospel, or, shall I say, to go back to the old one?"

"And that is——?"

"To present Christ in practical life as the living Master and King and example, and to apply Christianity to the life of our own time."

The Prime Minister had not taken his eyes off him. "What does this mean?" he had asked himself, but he only smiled his difficult smile and began to talk lightly. If this creed applied to the individual it applied also to the State; but think of a cabinet conducting the affairs of a nation on the charming principle of "taking no thought for the morrow," and "loving your enemies," and "turning the other cheek," and "selling all and giving to the poor"!

John stuck to his guns. If the Christian religion could not be the ultimate authority to rule a Christian nation, it was only because we lacked faith and trusted too much to mechanical laws made by statesmen rather than to moral laws made by Christ. "Either the life of Christ, as the highest standard and example, means something or it means nothing. If something, let us try to follow it; but if nothing, then for God's sake let us put it away as a cruel, delusive, and damnable mummery!"

The Prime Minister continued to ask himself, "What is the key to this?" and to look at John as he would have looked at a problem that had to be solved, but he only went on smiling and talking lightly. It was true we said a prayer and took an oath on the Bible in the Houses of Parliament, but did anybody think for a moment that we intended to trust the nation to the charming romanticism of the politics of Jesus? As for the Church, it was founded on acts of Parliament, it was endowed and established by the State, its head was the sovereign, its clergy were civil servants who went to levées and hung on the edge of drawing-rooms and troubled the knocker of No. 10 Downing-Street. And as for Christ's laws—in this country they were interpreted by the Privy Council and were under the direct control of a State department. Still, it was a harmless superstition that we were a Christian nation. It helped to curb the masses of the people, and if that was what John was thinking of——

The Prime Minister paused and stopped.

"Tell me, my boy," touching John's arm, "do you intend yourself to live—in short, the—well, after the example of the life of Christ?"

"As far as my weak and vain and sinful nature will permit, uncle!"

"And in what way would you propose to apply your new idea of Christianity?"

"My experiment would be made on a social basis, sir, and first of all in relation to women." John was hot all over, and his face had flushed up to the eyes.

The Prime Minister glanced stealthily across the table, passed his thin hand across his forehead, and thought, "So that's how it is!" But John was deep in his theme and saw nothing. The present position of women was intolerable. Upon the well-being of women, especially of working women, the whole welfare of society rested. Yet what was their condition? Think of it—their dependence on man, their temptations, their rewards, their punishments! Three halfpence an hour was the average wage of a working woman in England!—and that in the midst of riches, in the heart of luxury, and with one easy and seductive means of escape from poverty always open. Ruin lay in wait for them, and was beckoning them and enticing them in the shape of dancing houses and music halls and rich and selfish men.

"Not one man in a million, sir, would come through such an ordeal unharmed. And yet what do we do?—what does the Church do for these brave creatures on whose virtue and heroism the welfare of the nation depends? If they fall it cuts them off, and there is nothing before them but the streets or crime or the Union or suicide. And meanwhile it marries the men who have tempted them to the snug and sheltered darlings for whose wealth or rank or beauty they have been pushed aside. Oh, uncle, when I walk down Regent Street in the daytime I am angry, but when I walk down Regent Street at night I am ashamed. And then to think of the terrible solitude of London to working girls who want to live pure lives—the terrible spiritual loneliness!"

John's voice was breaking, but the Prime Minister had almost ceased to hear. Thinking he had realized the truth at last, his own youth seemed to be sitting before him and he felt a deep pity.

"Coffee here or in the library, your lordship?" said the man at his elbow.

"The library," he answered, and taking John's arm again he returned to the other room. There was a fire burning now, and a book lay under the lamp on a little table, with a silver paper-cutter through the middle to mark the page.

"How you remind me of your mother sometimes, John! That was just like her voice, do you know—just!"

Two hours afterward he led John Storm down the long corridor to the hall. His bleak face looked soft and his deep voice had a slight tremor. "Good-night, my dear boy, and remember your money is always waiting for you. Until your Christian social state is established you are only an advocate of socialism, and may fairly use your own. If yours is the Christianity of the first century it has to exist in the nineteenth, you know. You can't live on air or fly without wings. I shall be curious to see what approach, to the Christian ideal the condition of civilization admits of. Yet I don't know what your religious friends and the humdrum herd will think of you—mad probably, or at least weak and childish and perhaps even a hunter after easy popularity. But good-night, and God bless you in, your people's church and Devil's Acre!"

John was flushed and excited. He had been talking of his plans, his hopes, his expectations. God would provide for him in this as in everything, and then God's priest ought to be God's poor. Meantime two gentlemen in plush waited for him at the door. One handed him his hat, the other his stick and gloves.

Then with regular steps, and his hands behind him, the Prime Minister paced back through the quiet corridors. Returning to the library, he took up his book and tried to read. It was a novel, but he could not attend to the incidents in other people's lives. From time to time he said to himself: "Poor boy! Will he find her? Will he save her?" One pathetic idea had fixed itself on his mind—John Storm's love of God was love of a woman, and she was fallen and wrecked and lost.

A fortnight later John wrote to Glory:

"Fairly under weigh at last, dear Glory! Taken priest's orders, got the Bishop's 'license to officiate,' and found myself a church. It is St. Mary Magdalene's, Crown Street, Soho, a district that has borne for three hundred years the name of the 'Devil's Acre,' bears it still, and deserves it. The church is an old proprietary place, licensed, not consecrated, formerly belonging to Greek, or Italian, or French, or some other refugees, but long shut up and now much out of repair. Present owners, a company of Greek merchants, removed from Soho to the City, and being too poor (as trustees) to renovate the structure, they have forced me to get money for that purpose from my uncle, the Prime Minister. But the money is my own, apparently, my uncle having in my interest demanded from my father ten thousand pounds out of my mother's dowry, and got it. And now I am spending two thousand on the repair of my church buildings, notwithstanding the protests of the Prime Minister, who calls me 'chaplain to the Greek-Turks,' and of Mrs. Callender, who has discovered that I am a 'maudlin, sentimental, daft young spendthrift.' Dare say I am all that and a good deal more, as the wise world counts wisdom—but it matters little!

"Have not waited for the workmen, though, to begin operations. Took first services last Sunday. No organist, no choir, no clerk, and next to no congregation. Just the church cleaner, a good, simple old soul named Pincher, her son, a reformed drunkard and pawnbroker, and another convert who is a club waiter. Nevertheless, I went through the whole service, morning and evening, prayers, psalms, and sermon. God will be the more glorified.

"Have started my new crusade on behalf of women, too, and made various processions of three persons through the streets of Soho. First, my pawnbroker bearing the banner (a white cross, the object of various missiles), next my waiter carrying a little harmonium, and familiarly known as the 'organ man,' and finally myself in my cassock. Last mentioned proves to be a highly popular performance, being generally understood to be a man in a black petticoat. We have had a nightly accompaniment of a much larger procession, though, calling themselves 'Skellingtons,' otherwise the 'Skeletons,' an army of low women and roughs; who live vulture lives on this poor, soiled, grimy, forgotten world. Thank God, the ground of evil-doers is in danger, and they know it!

"Behind my church, in a dark, unwholesome alley called. Crook Lane, we have a clergy house, at present let out in tenements, the cellar being occupied as a gin shop. As soon as these premises can be cleared of their encumbrances I shall turn them into a club for working girls. Why not? In the old days the Church came to the people: let it come to the people now. Here we are in the midst of this mighty stronghold of the devil's kingdom of sin and crime. Foreign clubs, casinos, dancing academies, and gambling houses are round about us. What are we to do? Put up a forest of props (as at the Abbey) and keep off touch and contamination? God forbid! Let us go down into these dens of moral disease and disinfect them. The poor working girls, of Soho want their Sunday: give it them. They want music and singing: give it them. They want dancing: give them that also, for God's sake, give it them in your churches, or the devil will give it them in his hells!

"Expect to be howled at of course. Some good people will think I am either a fanatic or an artful schemer, while the clerical place-seekers, who love the flesh-pots of Egypt and have their eyes on the thrones of the Church and the world, will denounce my 'secularity' and tell me I am feeding the 'miry troughs' of the publican and sinner. No matter, if only God is pleased to vouchsafe 'signs following.' And one weary-faced lonely girl, grown fresh of countenance and happy of mien, or one bright little woman, snatched from the brink of perdition, will be a better fruit, of religion than some of them have seen for many a year.

"As soon as the workmen have cleared out I am going to establish a daily service and keep the church open always. Still at Mrs. Callender's, you see; but I am refusing all invitations, except as a priest, and already I don't seem to, have time to draw my breath. No income connected with St. Mary Magdalene's, or next to none, just enough to pay the caretaker; but I must not complain of that, for it is the accident to which I owe my church, nobody else wanting it under the circumstances. I had begun to think my time in the monastery wasted, but God knew better. It will help me to live the life of poverty, of purity, of freedom from the world.

"Love to the grandfather and the ladies. How I wish you were with me in the thick of the fight! Sometimes I dream you are, too, and I fancy I see you in the midst of these bright young things with their flowers and feathers—they will make beautiful Christians yet! Oddly enough, on the day you travelled to the island, every hour that took you farther away seemed to bring you nearer. Greetings!"

CHAPTER VII

"Glenfaba, 'the Oilan.'

"Oh, gracious and grateful friend, at length you have remembered the existence of the 'poor lone crittur' living in dead-alive land! Only that I lack gall to make oppression bitter, I should of course return your belated epistle by the Dead Letter Office, marked 'Unknown' across your 'Dear Glory,' there being no longer anybody in these regions who has a plausible claim to that dubious title. But, alas! I am not my own woman now, and with tears of shame I acknowledge that *any* letter from London comes like an angel's whisper breathed to me through the air.

"I dare say you have been unreasonable enough to think that I ought to have written to tell you of my arrival; and knowing that man is born to vanity as the sparks fly upward, I have more than once intended to take pen in hand and write; but there is something so sleepy in this island atmosphere that my good resolution has hitherto been a stillborn babe that has breathed but never cried!

"Know then that my journey hither was performed with due celerity and no further disaster than befalls me when, as usual, I have *done* those things which I ought not to have done, and left *undone* those things which I ought to have done—the former in this instance having reference to various bouts of crying—which drew forth the sympathy of a compassionate female sharper in the train—and the latter to the catch of my sachel, which enabled that obliging person to draw forth my embroidered pocket-handkerchief in exchange.

"I was in good time for the steamboat at Liverpool, and it was crowded, according to its wont, with the Lancashire lads and lasses, in whom affection is as contagious as the mumps. Being in the dumps myself on sailing out of the river, and thinking of the wild excitement with which I had sailed into it, I think I should have found that I had not *done* crying in both senses but for the interest of watching an amiable Bob Brierley who, with his arm about the waist of the person sitting next to him, kept looking round at the rest of the world from time to time with the innocence of one whose left hand didn't know what his right hand was doing.

"But we had hardly crossed the bar when the prince of the powers of the air began to envy the happiness of these dear young goodies, and if you had seen the weather for the next four hours you would have agreed that the devil must have had a hand in it! Up came a wave over the after quarter and down went the passengers below decks, staggering and screaming like brewery rats, and then on we came like the Israelites out of Egypt on eagles' wings! Having lost my own sea legs a little I thought it prudent to go down too, with my doggie tucked under my arm, and finding a berth in the ladies' cabin, I fell asleep and didn't awake until we were in the cross-current just off the island, when, amid moans and groans and other noises, I heard the tearful voice of a sick passenger asking, 'Is there any hope, stewardess?'

"The train got to Peel as the sun was setting behind the grim old castle walls, and when I saw the dear little town again I dropped half a tear, and even felt an insane desire to run out to meet it. Grandfather was at the station with old 'Caesar' and the pony carriage, and when I had done kissing him and he had done panting and puffing and talking nonsense, as if I had been Queen Victoria and the Empress of the French rolled into one, I could have cried to see how small and feeble he had become since I went away. We could not get off immediately, for in his simple joy at my return he was hailing everybody and everybody was hailing him, and the dear old Pharisee was sounding his trumpet so often in the market-place, that he might have glory of men, that I thought we should never get up to Glenfaba that night. When we did so at length the old aunties were waiting at the gate, and then he broke into exclamations again. 'Hasn't she grown tall? Look at her! Hasn't she, now?' Whereupon the aunties took up their parable with, 'Well, well! Aw, well! Aw, well now! Well, ye navar!' So that by the time I got through I had kissed everybody a dozen times, and was as red over the eyes as a grouse.

"Then we went into the house, and for the first five minutes I couldn't tell what had come over the old place to make it look so small and mean. It was just as if the walls of the rooms had been the bellows of a concertina and somebody had suddenly shut them. But there was the long clock clucking away on the landing, and there was Sir Thomas Traddles purring on the hearth-rug, and there were the same plates on the dresser, and the same map of Africa over the fireplace, with a spot of red ink where my father died.

"The moon was glistening on the sea when I went to bed that night, and when I got up in the morning the sun was shining on it, and a crow cut across my window cawing, and I heard grandfather humming to himself on the path below. And after my long spell in London, and my railway journey of the day before, it was the same as if I had fallen asleep in a gale on the high seas and awakened in a quiet harbour somewhere.

"So here I am, back at Glenfaba, in my old little room with my old little bed, and everything exactly as it used to be; and I begin to believe that when you went into that monastery you only just got the start of me in being dead. There used to be a few people in this place, but now there doesn't seem to be a dog left. All the youngsters have 'gone foreign,' and all the oldsters have gone to—'goodness knows which.' Sometimes we hear the bleat of sheep on the mountains, and sometimes the scream of seagulls overhead, and sometimes we hold a convocation of all living rooks in the elms on the lawn. We take no thought for the morrow, what we shall eat or what we shall put on, and on Sundays when the church bell rings we go out, like the Israelites in the wilderness, in clothes which wax not old after forty years. During the rest of the week we watch the blue-bottles knocking their stupid heads against the ceiling, and listen to the grasshoppers whispering in the grass, and fall asleep to the hum of the bees, and awake to the *hee-haw* of old Neilus's 'canary.' [* Donkey] Such is the dead-alive life we live at Glenfaba, and the days of our years are threescore years and ten, and if.... Ohoy! (A yawn.)

"I suppose it is basely ungrateful of me to talk like this, for the dear place itself is lovely enough to disturb one's hope of paradise, and this very morning is as fresh as the dew on the grass, with the larks singing above, and the river singing below, and clouds like little curls of foam hovering over the sea. And as for my three dear old dunces, who love me so much more than I deserve, I am ashamed in my soul when I overhear them planning good things for me to eat, and wild excitements for me to revel in, that I may not be dull or miss the luxuries I am accustomed to. 'Do you know I'm afraid Glory doesn't care so much for pinjane after all,' I heard grandfather whispering to Aunt Anna one morning, and half an hour afterward he was reproving Aunt Rachel for pressing me too hard to serve at the soup kitchen.

"They govern me like a child in pinafores, and of course like a child I revenge myself by governing all the house. But, oh, dear! oh, dear! gone are the days when I could live on water-gruel and be happy in a go-cart. Yes, the change is in me, not in them or the old home, and what's the good of putting back the clock when the sun is so stubbornly keeping pace? I might be happy enough at Glenfaba still, if I could only bring back the days when the garden trees were my gymnasium and I used to rock myself and sing like a bird on a bough in the wind, or when I led a band of boys to rob our own orchard—a bold deed, for which Bishop Anna ofttimes launched at me and! all her suffragans her severest censure—it was her slipper, I remember. But I can't run barefoot all day long on the wet sand now, with the salt spray blowing in my face, and a young lady of one-and-twenty seldom or never rushes out to play dumps and baggy-mug in public with little girls of ten.

"As a result, my former adventures are now limited to careering on the back of little 'Caesar,' who has grown so ancient and fat that he waddles like an old duck, and riding him is like working your passage. So I confine myself to sitting on committees, and being sometimes sat upon, and rubbing the runes for grandfather, and cleaning the milkpails for Aunt Anna, and even such holy kill-times as going to church regularly and watching Neilus when he is passing round the plate after 'Let your light so shine before men'—light to his practical intellect being clearly a synonym for silver in the shape of threepenny bits!

"But, oh my! oh my! I am a dark character in this place for all that The dear old goodies have never yet said a syllable about my letter announcing that I had gone over to the enemy (i. e., Satan and the music hall), and there is a dead hush in the house as often as the wind of conversation veers in that direction. This is nothing, though, to the white awe in the air when visitors call and I am questioned how I earn my living in London. I hardly know whether to laugh or cry at the long-drawn breath of relief when I wriggle out of a tight place without telling a lie. But you can't hide an eel in a sack, and I know the truth will pop out one of these days. Only yesterday I went district-visiting with Aunt Rachel, and one of the Balaams of life, who keeps a tavern for fishermen, lured us into his bar parlour to look at a portrait of 'Gloria' which he had cut out of an illustrated paper and pinned up on the wall 'because it resembled me so much!' Oh, dear! oh, dear! I could have found it in my heart to brazen it out on the spot at this sight of my evil fame; but when I saw poor little auntie watching me with fearful eyes I talked away like a mill-wheel and went out thanking God that the rest of the people of Peel were not as other men are, or even as this publican.

"I have been getting newspapers myself, though, sent by my friend Rosa; and as long as the mis-reporters concerned themselves with my own doings and failures to do, and lied as tenderly as an epitaph about my disappearance from London, I cut them up and burned them. But when they forgot me, and began to treat of other people's triumphs, I made Neilus my waste-paper basket, on the understanding that the papers were to go to the fishermen just home from Kinsale. Then from time to time he told me they were 'goin' round, miss, goin' round,' and gave me other assurances of 'the greatest circulation in the world,' which was true enough certainly, though the old thief omitted to say it was at the paper-mill, where they were being turned into pulp.

"But, heigho! I don't need newspapers to remind me of London. Like St. Paul, I have a devil that beats me with fists, and as often as a clear day comes, and one can see things a long way off, he makes me climb to the top of Slieu Whallin [* A mountain in Man.] that I may sit on the beacon by the hour and strain my eyes for a glimpse of England, feeling like Lot's wife when she looked back on her old home, and then coming down with a heavy heart and a taste of tears in my mouth as if I had been turned into a pillar of salt. Dear old London! But I suppose it is going on its way just as it used to do, with its tides of traffic and its crowds and carriages, and wandering merchants and hawkers crying their wares, and everything the same as ever, just the same, although Glory isn't there!"

"10.30 P. M.—I had to interrupt the writing of my letter this morning owing to an alarm of illness seizing grandfather. He had been taken with a sudden faintness. Of course we sent for the doctor, but before he arrived the faintness had passed, so he looked wise at us, like a prize riddle which had to be guessed before his next visit, left us his autograph (a wonderful hieroglyphic), and went away. Since then grandfather has been in the hands of a less taciturn practitioner, whom he calls the 'flower of Glenfaba' (that's me), and after talking nonsense to him all day and playing chess with him all the evening I have to put him to bed laughing, and come back to my own room to finish my letter with an easier mind. For the last half-hour the aurora has been pulsing in the northern sky, and I have been thinking that the glorious phantasmagoria must be the sign of a gale in heaven, just as sleet and mist and black wind are the signs of a gale on earth. But it has tripped off into nothingness and only the dark night is left, through which the dogs at Knockaloe are keeping up their private correspondence with the dogs at Ballamoar by the medium of their nightly howls.

"Oh, dear! Only 10.30! And to know that while we are going to bed by country hours, with nearly everything still and dead around us, London is just beginning to bestir itself! When I lie down and try to sleep I shall see the wide squares, with their statues of somebody inside, and the blaze of lights over the doors of the theatres, and all the tingling life of the great and wonderful city. Ugh! It makes one feel like one's own ghost wandering through the upper rooms and across the dark landings, and hearing the strains of the music and the sounds of the dancing from the ballroom below stairs!

"But, my goodness! (I can still swear on that, you see, and not be forsworn!) 'What's the odds if you're jolly?—and I allus is!' How's your dog? Mine would write you a letter, only her heart is moribund, and if things go on as they are going she must set about making her will. In fact, she is now lying at the foot of my bed thinking matters out, and bids me tell you that after various attempts to escape Home Rule, not being (like her mistress) one of those natures made perfect through suffering, she is only 'kept alive by the force of her own volition,' in this house that is full of old maids and has nothing better in it than one old cat, and he isn't worth hunting, being destitute of a tail. Naturally she is doing her best (like somebody else) to keep herself unspotted from that world which is a source of so much temptation, but she's bound to confess that a little 'divilment' now and then would help her to take a more holy and religious view of life.

"I 'wish you happy' in your new enterprise; but if you are going in for being the champion of woman in this world—of her wrongs—I warn you not to be too pointed in your moral, for there is a story here of a handsome young curate who was so particular in the pulpit with 'Lovest thou me' that a lady followed him into the vestry and admitted that she did. Soberly, it is a great and noble effort, and I've half a mind to love you for it. If men want women to be good they *will* be good, for women dance to the tune that men like best, and always have done so since the days of Adam—not forgetting that gentleman's temptation, nor yet his excuse about 'the woman *Thou gavest* me,' which shows he wasn't much of a husband anyway, though certainly he hadn't much choice of a wife.

"My love to dear old London! Sometimes I have half a mind to skip off and do my wooing myself. Perhaps I should do so, only that Rosa writes that she would like to come and spend her summer holiday in Peel. Haven't I told you about Rosa? She's the lady journalist that Mr. Drake introduced me to.

> "*But let's to bed,*
>
> *Said Sleepyhead.*

"Glory.

"P.S.—IMPORTANT. Ever since I left London I have been tormented with the recollection of poor Polly's baby. She put him out to nurse with the Mrs. Jupe you heard of, and that person put him out to somebody else. While the mother lived I had no business to interfere, but I can't help thinking of the motherless mite now and wondering what has become of him. I suppose that like Jeshurun he waxeth fat and kicketh by this time, yet it would be the act of a man and a clergyman if anybody would take up my neglected duty and make it his business to see that there is somebody to love the poor child. Mrs. Jupe's address is 5a, The Little Turnstile, going from Holborn into Lincoln's Inn Fields."

CHAPTER VIII

It was on a Saturday morning that John Storm received Glory's letter, and on the evening of the same day he set out in search of Mrs. Jupe's. The place was not easy to find, and when he discovered it at length he felt a pang at the thought that Glory herself had lived in this dingy burrowing. As he was going up to the door of the little tobacco shop a raucous voice within was saying, "That's what's doo on the byeby, and till you can py up you needn't be a-kemmin' 'ere no more." At the next moment a young woman crossed him on the threshold. She was a little slender thing, looking like a flower that has been broken by the wet. He recognised her as the girl who had nursed the baby in Cook Lane on the day of his first visit to Soho. She was crying, and to hide her swollen eyes she dropped her head at passing, and he saw her faded ribbons and soiled straw hat.

A woman of middle age behind the counter was curtsying to his clerical attire, and a little girl at the door of an inner room was looking at him out of the corner of her eyes, with head aslant.

"Father Storm, I think, sir. Come in and set you down, sir.—Mind the shop, Booboo.—My 'usband 'as told me about ye, sir. 'You'll know 'im at onct, Lidjer,' 'e sez, siz 'e.—No, 'e ain't 'ome from the club yet, but 'e might be a-kemmin' in any time now, sir."

John Storm had seated himself in the little dark parlour, and was looking round and thinking of Glory. "No matter; my business is with you, Mrs. Jupe," he answered, and at that the twinkling eyes and fat cheeks, which had been doing their best to smile, took on a look of fear.

"Wot's the metter?" she asked, and she closed the door to the shop.

"Nothing, I trust, my good woman," and then he explained his errand.

Mrs. Jupe listened attentively and seemed to be asking herself who had sent him.

"The poor young mother is dead now, as you may know, and——"

"But the father ain't," said the woman sharply, "and, begging your parding, sir, if 'e wants ter know where the byeby is 'e can come 'isself and not send sembody else!"

"If the child is well, my good woman, and well cared for——"

"It *is* well keered for, and it's gorn to a pusson I can trust."

"Then what have you got to conceal? Tell me where it is, and——"

"Not me! If it's 'is child, and 'e wants it, let 'im py for it, and interest ep ter dite. Them swells is too fond of gettin' parsons to pull their chestnuts out o' the fire."

"If you suppose I am here in the interests of the father, you are mistaken, I do assure you."

"Ow, you do, do yer?"

Matters had reached this pass when the door opened and Mr. Jupe came in. Off went his hat with a respectful salutation, but seeing the cloud on his wife's face, he abridged his greeting. The woman's apron was at her eyes in an instant.

"Wot's gowin' on?" he asked. John Storm tried to explain, but the woman contented herself with crying.

"Well, it's like this, don'cher see, Father. My missis is that fond of childring, and it brikes 'er 'eart——"

Was the man a fool or a hypocrite?

"Mr. Jupe," said John, rising, "I'm afraid your wife has been carrying on an improper and illegal business."

"Now stou thet, sir," said the man, wagging his head. "I respects the Reverend Jawn Storm a good deal, but I respects Mrs. Lidjer Jupe a good deal more, and when it comes to improper and illegal bizniss——"

"Down't mind 'im, 'Enery," said the wife, now weeping audibly.

"And down't you tyke on so, Lidjer," said the husband, and they looked as if they were about to embrace.

John Storm could stand no more. Going down the court he was thinking with a pang of Glory—that she had lived months in the atmosphere of that impostor—when somebody touched his arm in the darkness. It was the girl. She was still crying.

"I reckerlec' seeing you in Crook Lane, sir, the day we christened my byeby, and I waited, thinking p'raps you could help me."

"Come this way," said John, and walking by his side along the blank wall of Lincoln's Inn Fields, the girl told her story. She lived in one room of the clergy-house at the back of his church. Having to earn her living, she had answered an advertisement in a Sunday paper, and Mrs. Jupe had taken her baby to nurse. It was true she had given up all claim to the child, but she could not help going to see it—the little one's ways were so engaging. Then she found that Mrs. Jupe had let it out to somebody else. Only for her "friend" she might never have heard of it again. He had found it by accident at a house in Westminster. It was a fearful place, where men went for gambling. The man who kept it had just been released from eighteen months' imprisonment, and the wife had taken to nursing while the husband was in prison. She was a frightful woman, and he was a shocking man, and "they knocked the children about cruel." The neighbours heard screams and slaps and moans, and they were always crying "Shame!" She had wanted to take her own baby away, but the woman would not give it up because there were three weeks' board owing, and she could not pay.

"Could you take me to this house, my child?"

"Yes, sir."

"Then come round to the church after service to-morrow night."

The girl's tearful face glistened like April sunshine.

"And will you help me to get my little girl? Oh, how good you are! Everybody is saying what a Father it is that's come to——" She stopped, then said quite soberly: "I'll get somebody to lend me a shawl to bring 'er 'ome in. People say they pawn everything, and perhaps the beautiful white perlice I bought for 'er ... Oh, I'll never let 'er out of my sight again, never!"

"What is your name, my girl?"

"Agatha Jones," the girl answered.

It was nearly eleven o'clock on Sunday night before they were ready to start on their errand. Meantime Aggie had done two turns at the foreign clubs, and John Storm had led a procession through Crown Street and been hit by a missile thrown by a "Skeleton," whom he declined to give in charge. At the corner of the alley he stopped to ask Mrs. Pincher to wait up for him, and the girl's large eyes caught sight of the patch of plaster above his temple.

"Are you sure you want to go, sir?" she said.

"There's no time to lose," he answered. The bloodhound was with him; he had sent home for it since the attempted riot.

As they walked toward Westminster she told him where she had been, and what money she had earned. It was ten shillings, and that would buy so many things for baby.

"To-morrow I'll get a cot for her—one of those wicker ones; iron is so expensive. She'll want a pair o' socks too, and by-and-bye she'll 'ave to be shortened."

John Storm was thinking of Glory. He seemed to be retreading the steps of her life in London. The dog kept close at his heels.

"She'll 'a bin a month away now, a month to-morrow. I wonder if she's grow'd much—I wonder! It's wrong of people letting their childring go away from them. I'll never go out at nights again—not if I 'ave to tyke in sewin' for the slop shops. See this?" laughing nervously and showing a shawl that hung on her arm. "It's to bring 'er 'ome in—the nights is so chill for a byeby."

John's heart was heavy at sight of these little preparations, but the young mother's face was radiant.

As they went by the Abbey, under its forest of scaffolding, and, walking toward Millbank, dipped into the slums, that lie in the shadow of the dark prison, they passed soldiers from the neighbouring barracks going arm-in-arm with girls, and this made Aggie talk of her "friend," and cry a little, saying it was a week since she had seen him, and she was afraid he must have 'listed. She knew he was rude to people sometimes, and she asked pardon for him, but he wasn't such a bad boy, after all, and he never knocked you about except when he was drinking.

The house they were going to was in Angel Court, and having its door only to the front, it was partly sheltered from observation. A group of women with their aprons over their heads stood talking in whispers at the corner. One of them recognised Aggie and asked if she had got her child yet, whereupon John stopped and made some inquiries. The goings-on at the house were scandalous. The men who went to it were the lowest of the low, and there was scarcely one of them who hadn't "done time." The man's name was Sharkey, and his wife was as bad as he was. She insured the children at seven pounds apiece, and "Lawd love ye, sir, at that price the poor things is worth more dead nor alive!"

Aggie's face was becoming white, and she was touching John Storm's elbow as if pleading with him to come away, but he asked further questions. Yes, there were several children. A twelve-months' baby, a boy, was fretful with his teething, and on Sunday nights, when the woman was wanted downstairs, she just put the poor darling to bed and locked the room. If you lived next door, you could hear his crying through the wall.

"Agatha," said John, as they stepped up to the door, "get us both into this house as best you can, then leave the rest to me.—Don, lie close!"

Aggie tapped at the door. A little slide in it was run back and a voice said, "Who's there?"

"Aggie," the girl answered.

"Who's that with you?"

"A friend of Charlie's," and then the door was opened.

John crossed the threshold first, the dog followed him, the girl entered last. When the door had closed behind them, the doorkeeper, a young man holding a candle in his hand, was staring at John with his whole face open.

"Hush! Not a word!—Don, watch that man!"

The young man looked at the dog and turned pale.

"Where is Mrs. Sharkey?"

"Downstairs, sir."

There were sounds of men's voices from below, and from above there came the convulsive sobs of a child, deadened as by a door between.

"Give me your candle."

The man gave it.

"Don't speak or stir, or else——"

John glanced at the dog, and the man trembled.

"Come upstairs, child," and the girl followed him to the upper floor.

On reaching the room in which the baby was crying they tried the door. It was locked. John attempted to force it, but it would not yield. The child's sobs were dying down to a sleepy moan.

Another room stood open and they went in. It was the living-room. A kettle on the fire was singing and puffing steam. There was no sign of a key anywhere. Only a table, some chairs, a disordered sofa, certain sporting newspapers lying about, and a few pictures on the walls. Some of the pictures were of race-horses, but all the rest were memorial cards, and one bore the text, "He shall gather them in his arms." Aggie was shuddering as with cold, being chilled by some unknown fear.

"We must go down to the cellar—there's no help for it," said John.

The man in the hall had not spoken or stirred. He was still gazing in terror on the bloodshot eyes looking out of the darkness. John gave the candle to the girl and began to go noiselessly downstairs. There was not a movement in the house now. Big Ben was striking. It was twelve o'clock.

At the next moment John Storm was midway down, and had full view of the den. It was a washing cellar with a coal vault going out of it under the street. Some fifteen or twenty men, chiefly foreigners, were gathered about a large table covered with green baize, on which a small lamp was burning. A few of the men were seated on chairs ranged about, the others were standing at the back in rows two deep. They were gambling. The game was faro. Rows of lucifer matches were laid on the table, half-crowns were staked on them, and cards were cut and dealt. Except the banker, a middle-aged man with the wild eye of the hard spirit-drinker, everybody had his face turned away from the cellar stairs.

They did not smoke or drink, and they only spoke to each other when the stakes were being received or paid. Then they quarrelled and swore in English. After that there was a chilling and hideous silence, as if something awful were about to occur. The lamp cast a strong light on the table, but the rest of the room was darkened by patches of shadow.

The coal vault had been turned into a drinking-bar, and behind the counter there was a well-stocked stillage. In the depths of its shade a woman sat knitting. She had a gross red and white face, and in the arch above her was the iron grid in the pavement. Somebody on the street walked over it, causing a hollow sound as of soil falling on a coffin.

John Storm was no coward, but a certain tremor passed over him on finding himself in this subterranean lurking-place of men who were as beasts. He stood a full minute unseen. Then he heard the woman say in a low hiss, "Cat's mee-e-et!" and he knew he had been observed. The men turned and looked at him, not suddenly, or all at once, but furtively, cautiously, slowly. The banker crouched at the table with an astonished face and tried to smuggle the cards out of sight.

John stood calmly, his whole figure displaying courage and confidence. The group of men broke up. "He's got the 'coppers,'" said one. Nobody else spoke, and they began to melt away. They disappeared through a door at the back which led into a yard, for, like rats, the human vermin always have a second way out of their holes.

In half a minute the cellar was nearly empty. Only the banker and the woman and one young man remained. The young man was Charlie.

"What cheer, myte?" he said with an air of unconcern. "Is it trecks ye want, sir? Here ye are then," and he threw a pack of cards at John's feet.

"It's that gel o' yawn that's done this," said the woman.

"So it's a got-up thing, is it?" said Charlie, and stepping to the counter, he took up a drinking-glass, broke it at the rim; and holding its jagged edges outward, turned to use it as a weapon.

John Storm had not yet spoken, but a magnetic instinct warned him. He whistled, and the dog bounded down. The young man threw his broken glass on the floor and cried to the keeper of the house: "Don't stir, you! First you know, the beast will be at yer throat!"

Hearing Charlie's voice, Aggie was creeping down the stairs. "Charlie!" she cried. Charlie threw open his coat, stuck his fingers in the armholes of his waistcoat, said in a voice of hatred, passion, and rage, "Go and pawn yourself!" and then swaggered out at the back door. The keeper made show of following, but John Storm called on him to stop. The man looked at the dog and obeyed. "Wot d'ye want o' me?" he said.

"I want this girl's baby. That's the first thing I want. I'll tell you the rest afterward."

"Oh, that's it, is it?" The man's grimace was frightful.

"It's gone, sir. We've lost it," said the woman, with a hideous expression.

"That story will not pass with me, my good woman. Go upstairs and unlock the door! You too, my man, go on!"

A minute later they were in a bedroom above. Three neglected children lay asleep on bundles of rags. One of twelve months' old was in a wicker cradle, one of three years was in a wooden cot, and a younger child was in a bed. Aggie had come up behind, and stood by the door trembling and weeping.

"Now, my girl, find your baby," said John, and the young mother hurried with eager eyes from the cradle to the cot and from the cot to the bed.

"Yes, here it is," she cried. "No—oh no, no!" and she began to wring her hands.

"Told yer so," said the woman, and with a wicked grin she pointed to a memorial card which hung on the wall.

Aggie's child was dead and buried. Diarrhoea! The doctor at the dispensary had given a certificate of death, and Charlie had shared the insurance money. "Wish to Christ it was ended!" he had said. He had been drunk ever since.

The poor girl was stunned. She was no longer crying. "Oh, oh, oh! What shall I do?" she said.

"Who's child is this?" said John, standing over the wicker cradle. The little sufferer from inflamed gums had sobbed itself to sleep.

"A real laidy's," said the woman. "Mrs. Jupe told us to tyke great kear of it. The father is Lord something."

"My poor girl," said John, turning to Aggie, "could you carry this child home for me?"

"Oh, oh, oh!" said the girl, but she wrapped the shawl about the child and lifted it up sleeping.

"Now, you down't!" said the man, putting himself on guard before the door. "That child is worth 'undrids of pounds to me, and——"

"Stand back, you brute!" said John, and with the girl and her burden he passed out of the house.

The front door stood open and the neighbourhood had been raised. Trollopy women in their under-petticoats and with their hair hanging about their necks were gathered at the end of the court. Aggie was crying again, and John pushed through the crowd without speaking.

They went back by Broad Sanctuary, where a solitary policeman was pacing to and fro on the echoing pavement. Big Ben was chiming the half-hour after midnight. The child coughed like a sheep constantly, and Aggie kept saying, "Oh, oh, oh!"

Mrs. Pincher, in her widow's cap and white apron, was waiting up for them, and John committed the child to her keeping. Then he said to Aggie, who was turning away, "My poor child, you have suffered deeply, but if you will leave this man I will help you to begin life again, and if you want money I will find it."

"Well, he *is* a Father and no mistake!" said Mrs. Pincher; but the girl only answered in a hopeless voice, "I don't want no money, and I don't want to begin life again."

As she crossed the court to her room in the tenement house they heard her "Oh, oh, oh!"

Before going to bed that night John Storm wrote to Glory:

"Hurrah! Have got poor Polly's baby, so you may set your heart at ease about it. All the days of my life I have been thought to be a dreamer, but it is surprising what a man can do when he sets to work for somebody else! Your former landlady turns out to be the wife of my 'organ man,' and it was pitiful to see the dear old simpleton's devotion to his bogus little baggage. I have lost him, of course, but that was unavoidable.

"It was by help of another victim that I traced the child at last. She is a ballet girl of some sort, and it was as much as I could stand to see the poor young thing carrying Polly's baby, her own being dead and buried without a word said to her. Short of the grace of God she will go to the bad now. Oh, when will the world see that in dealing with the starved hearts of these poor fallen creatures God Almighty knows best how to do his own business? Keep the child with the mother, foster the maternal instinct, and you build up the best womanhood. Drag them apart, and the child goes to the dogs and the mother to the devil.

"But Polly's baby is safely lodged with Mrs. Pincher, a dear old grandmotherly soul who will love it like her own, and all the way home I have been making up my mind to start baby-farming myself on fresh lines. He who wrongs the child commits a crime against the State. However low a woman has fallen, she is a subject of the Crown, and if she is a mother she is the Crown's creditor. These are my first principles, the application will come anon. Meantime you have given me a new career, a glorious mission! Thank God and Glory Quayle for it for ever and ever! Then—who knows?—perhaps you will come back and take it up yourself some day. When I think of the precious time I spent, in that monastery ... but no, only for that I should not be here.

"Oh, life is wonderful! But I feel afraid that I shall wake up—perhaps in the streets somewhere—and find I have been dreaming. Deeply grieved to hear of the grandfather's attack. Trust it has passed. But if not, certain I am that all is well with him and that he is staid only on God.

"Hope you are well and plodding through this wilderness in comfort, avoiding the thorns as well as you can. Glenfaba may be dull, but you do well to keep out of the whirlpool of London for the present. Yours is a snug spot, and when storms are blowing even the sea-gulls shelter about your house, I remember ... But why Rosa? Is Peel the only place for a summer holiday?"

CHAPTER IX

"Glenfaba.

"Oh, my dear John Storm, is it coals of fire you are heaping on my head, or fire of brimstone? Your last letter with its torrents of enthusiasm came sweeping down on me like a flood. What work you are in the midst of! What a life! What a purpose! While I—I am lying here like an old slipper thrown up oil the sea-beach. Oh, the pity oft, the pity oft! It must be glorious to be in the rush and swirl of all this splendid effort, whatever comes of it! One's soul is thrilled, one's heart expands! As for me, the garden of my mind is withering, and I am consuming the seed I ought to sow.

"Rosa has come. She has been here a month nearly, and is just charming, say what you will. Her thoughts have the dash of the great world, and I love to hear her talk. True, she troubles me sometimes, but that's only my envy and malice and all uncharitableness. When she tells of Betty-this and Ellen-that, and their wonderful successes and triumphs, I'm the meanest sinner that crawls.

"It's funny to see how the old folk bear themselves toward her. Aunt Rachel regards her as a sort of an artist, and is clearly afraid that she will break out into madness in spots somewhere. Aunt Anna disapproves of her hair, which is brushed up like a man's, and of her skirt, which 'would be no worse if it were less like a pair of breeches,' for she has brought her 'bike.' She talks on dangerous subjects also, and nobody did such things in auntie's young days. Then she addresses the old girlies as I do, and calls grandfather 'G-rand-dad,' and like the witch of Endor generally, is possessed of a familiar spirit. Of course I give her various warning looks from time to time lest the fat should be in the fire, but she's a woman, bless her! and it's as true as ever it was that a woman can keep the secret she doesn't know.

"Yes, the ideal of womanhood has changed since the old aunties were young; but when I listen to Rosa and then look over at Rachel with her black ringlets, and at Anna with her old-fashioned 'front,' I shudder and ask myself, 'Why do I struggle?' What is the reward if one gives up the fascination of life and the world? There is no reward. Nothing but solitary old-maidism, unless two of you happen to be sisters, for who else will join her shame to yours? Dreams, dreams, only dreams of the dearest thing that ever comes into a woman's arms—and then you awake and there is no one there. A dame's school, when the old father is gone, but no children of your own to love you, nobody to think of you, scraping a little here, pinching a little there, growing older and smaller year by year, looking yellow and craned like an apple that has been kept on the top shelf too long, and then—the end!

"Oh, but I'm trying so hard, so very hard, to be 'true to the higher self in me,' because somebody says I must. What do you think I did last week? In my character of Lady Bountiful I gave an old folks' supper in the soup kitchen, understood to be in honour of my return. Roast beef and plum duff, not to speak of pipes and 'baccy, and forty old people of both sexes sitting down to 'the do.' After supper there was a concert, when Chaise (the fat old thief!) overflowed the 'elber' chair, and alluded to me as 'our beautiful donor,' and lured me into singing Mylecharaine, and leading the company, when we closed with the doxology.

"But 'it was not myself at all, Molly dear, 'twas my shadow on the wall,' and in any case man can't live by soup kitchens alone—nor woman either. And knowing what a poor, weak, vain woman I am at the best, I ask myself sometimes would it not be a thousand times better if I yielded to my true nature instead of struggling to realize a bloodless ideal that is not me in the least, but only my picture in the heart of some one who thinks me so much better than I am?

"Not that anybody ever sees what a hypocrite I can be, though I came near to letting the cat out of the bag as lately as last night. You must know that when I turned my back on London at the command of John Knox the second, I brought all my beautiful dresses along with me, except such of them as were left at the theatre. Yet I daren't lay them out in the drawers, so I kept them under lock and key in my boxes. There they lurked like evil spirits in ambush, and as often as their perfume escaped into the room my eyes watered for another sight of them! But in spite of all temptation I resisted, I conquered, I triumphed—until last night when Rosa talked of Juliet, what a glorious creature she was, and how there was nobody on the stage who could 'look' her and 'play' her too!

"What do you think I did? Shall I tell you? Yes, I will. I crept upstairs to my quiet little room, tugged the box from its hiding-place under the bed, drew out my dresses—my lovely, lovely brocades—and put them on! Then I spoke the potion speech, beginning in a whisper, but getting louder as I went on, and always looking at myself in the glass. I had blown out the candle, and there was no light in the room but the moon that was shining on my face, but I was glowing, my very soul was afire, and when I came to the end I drew myself up with eyes closed and head thrown back and heart that paused a beat or two, and said, '*I—I* am Juliet, for I am a great actress!'

"Oh, oh, oh! I could scream with laughter to think of what happened next! Suddenly I became aware of somebody knocking at my door (I had locked it) and of a thin voice outside saying fretfully: 'Glory, whatever is it? Aren't you well, Glory?' It was the little auntie; and thinking what a shock she would have if I opened the door and she came upon this grand Italian lady instead of poor little me, I had to laugh and to make excuses while I smuggled off my gorgeous things and got back into my plain ones!

"It was a narrow squeak; but I had a narrower one some days before. Poor grandfather! He regards Rosa as belonging to a superior race, and loves to ask her what she thinks of Glory. He has grown quite simple lately, and as soon as he thinks my back is turned he is always saying, 'And what is your opinion of my granddaughter, Miss Macquarrie?' To which she answers, 'Glory is going to make your name immortal, Mr. Quayle.' Then his eyes sparkle and he says, 'Do you think so?—do you really think so?' Whereupon she talks further balderdash, and the dear old darling smiles a triumphant smile!

"But I always notice that not long afterward his eyes look wet and his head hangs low, and he is saying to the aunties, with a crack in his voice: 'She'll go away again. You'll see she will. Her beauty and her talents belong to the world.' And then I burst in on them and scold them, and tell them not to talk nonsense.

"Nevertheless he is beginning to regard Rosa with suspicion, as if she were a witch luring me away, and one evening last week we had to steal into the garden to talk that we might escape from his watchful eyes. The sun had set—there was the red glow behind the castle across the sky and the sea, and we were walking on the low path by the river under the fuchsia hedge that hangs over from the lawn, you know. Rosa was talking with her impetuous dash of the great career open to any one who could win the world in London, how there were people enough to help her on, rich men to find her opportunities, and even to take theatres for her if need be. And I was hesitating and halting and stammering: 'Yes, yes, if it were the *regular* stage ... who knows? ... perhaps it might not be opened to the same objections, ...' when suddenly the leaves of the fuchsia rustled as with a gust of wind, and we heard footsteps on the path above.

"It was the grandfather, who had come out on Rachel's arm and overheard what I had said! 'It's Glory!' he faltered, and then I heard him take his snuff and blow his nose as if to cover his confusion, thinking I was deceiving them and carrying on a secret intercourse. I hardly know what happened next, except that for the five minutes following 'the great actress' had to talk with the tongues of men and angels (Beelzebub's) in order to throw dust in the dear old eyes and drive away their doubts. It was a magnificent performance, 'you go bail.' I'll never do the like of it again, though I had only one old man and one old maid and one young woman for audience. The house 'rose' at me too, and the poor old grandfather was appeased. But when we were back indoors I overheard him saying: 'After all there's no help for it. She's dull with us—what wonder! We can't cage our linnet, Rachel, and perhaps we shouldn't try. A song-bird came to cheer us, but it will fly away. We are only old folks, dear—it's no use crying.' And on going to his room that night he closed his door and said his prayers in a whisper, that I might not hear him when he sobbed.

"He hasn't left his bed since. I fear he never will More than once I have been on the point of telling him there is no reason to think the deluge would come if I *did*, go back to London; but I will never leave him now. Yet I wish Aunt Rachel wouldn't talk so much of the days when I went away before. It seems that every night, on his way to his own room, he used to step into my empty one and come out with his eyes dim and his lips moving. I am not naturally hard-hearted, but I can't love grandfather like that. Oh, the cruelty of life! ... I know it ought to be the other way about; ... but I can't help it.

"All the same I could cry to think how short life is, and how little of it I can spare. 'Cling fast to me and hold me,' my heart is always saying, but meantime London is calling to me, calling to me, like the sea, and I feel as if I were a wandering mermaid and she were my ocean home.

"Later.—Poor, poor grandfather! I was interrupted in the writing of my letter this morning by another of those sudden alarms. He had fainted again, and it is extraordinary how helpless the aunties are in a case of illness. Grandfather knows it too; and after I had done all I could to bring him round, he opened his eyes and whispered that he had something to say to me alone. At that the poor old things left the room with tears of woe and a look of understanding. Then fetching a difficult breath he said, '*You* are not afraid, Glory, are you?' and I answered him 'No,' though my heart was trembling. And then a feeble smile struggled through the wan features of his drawn face, and he told me his attack was only another summons. 'I'll soon die for good,' he said, 'and you must be strong and brave, my child, for death is the common lot, and then what is there to fear?' I didn't try to contradict him—what was the good of doing that? And after he had spoken of the coming time he talked quietly of his past life, how he had weathered the storm for seventy odd years, and his Almighty Father was bringing him into harbour at last. 'I can't pray for life any longer, Glory. Many a time I did so in the old days when I had to bring up my little granddaughter, but my task is over now, and after the day is done where is the tired labourer who does not lie down to his rest with a will?'

"The doctor has been and gone. There is no ailment, and nothing to be done or hoped. It is only a general failure and a sinking earthward of the poor worn-out body as the soul rises to the heaven that is waiting to receive it. What a pagan I feel beside him! And how glad I am that I didn't talk of leaving him again when he was on the eve of his far longer journey! I have sent the aunties to bed, but Rosa has made me promise to awaken her at four, that she may take her turn at his bedside.

"Next Morning.—Rosa relieved me during the night, and I came to my room and lay down in the dullness of the dawn. But now I am sorry that I allowed her to do so, for I did not sleep, and grandfather appears to have been troubled with dreams. I fancied he shuddered a little as I left them together, and more than once through the wall I heard him cry, 'Bring him back!' in the toneless voice of one who is labouring under the terrors of a nightmare. But each time I heard Rosa comforting him, so I lay down again without going in.

"Being stronger this morning, he has been propped up in bed writing a letter. When he called for the pens and paper I asked if I couldn't write it for him, but the old darling made a great mystery of the matter, and looked artful, and asked if it was usual to fight your enemy with his own powder and shot. Of course I humoured him and pretended to be mighty curious, though I think I know who the letter was written to, all the same that he kept the address side of the envelope hidden even when the front of it was being sealed. He sealed it with sealing-wax, and I held the candle while he did so, with his poor trembling fingers in danger from the light, and then I stamped it with my mother's pearl ring, and he smuggled it under the pillow.

"Since breakfast he has shown an increased inclination to doze, but there have been visits from the wardens and from neighbouring parsons, for a *locum tenens* has had to be appointed. Of course, they have all inquired where his pain is, and on being told that he has none, they have gone downstairs cackling and clucking and crowing in various versions of 'Praise God for that!' I hate people who are always singing the doxology.

"Noon.—Condition unchanged, except that in the intervals of drowsiness his mind has wandered a little. He appears to live in the past. Looking at me with conscious eyes, he calls me 'Lancelot'—my father's name. It has been so all the morning. One would think he was walking in a twilight land where he mistakes people's faces and the dead are as much alive as the living.

"They all think I am brave, oh, so brave! because I do not cry now, as everybody else does—even Aunt Anna behind her apron—although my tears can flow so easily, and at other times I keep them constantly on tap. But I am really afraid, and down at the bottom of my heart I am terrified. It is just as if *something* were coming into the house slowly, irresistibly, awfully, and casting its shadow on the floor already.

"I have found out the cause of his outcries in the night. Aunt Rachel says he was dreaming of my father's departure for Africa. That was twenty-two years ago, but it seems that the memory of the last day has troubled him a good deal lately. 'Don't you remember it?' he has been saying. 'There were no railways in the island then, and we stood at the gate to watch the coach that was taking him away. He sat on the top and waved his red handkerchief. And when he had gone, and it was no use watching, we turned back to the house—you and Anna and poor, pretty young Elise. He never came back, and when Glory goes again she'll never come back either.'

"In the intervals of his semi-consciousness, when he mistakes me for my father, my wonderful bravery often fails me, and I find excuses for going out of the room. Then I creep noiselessly through the house and listen at half-open doors. Just now I heard him talking quite rationally to Rachel, but in a voice that seemed to speak inwardly, not outwardly, as before. 'She can't help it, poor child!' he said. 'Some day she'll know what it is, but not yet, not until she has a child of her own. The race looks forward, not backward. God knew when he created us that the world couldn't go on without that bit of cruelty, and who am I that I should complain?'

"I couldn't bear it any longer, and with a pain at my heart I ran in and cried, 'I'll never leave you, grandfather.' But he only smiled and said, 'I'll not be keeping you long, Glory, I'll not be keeping you long,' and then I could have died for shame.

"Evening.—All afternoon he has been like a child, and everything present to his consciousness seems to have been reversed. The shadow of eternity appears to have wiped out time. When I have raised him up in bed he has delighted to think he was a little boy in his young mother's arms. Oh, sweet dream! The old man with his furrowed forehead and beautiful white head and all the heavy years rolled back! More than once he has asked me if he may play till bedtime, and I have stroked his wrinkled hands and told him 'Yes,' for I pretend to be his mother, who died, when she was old.

"But the 'part' is almost too much for me, and, lest I should break down under the strain of it, I am going out of his room constantly. I have just been into his study. It is as full as ever of his squeezes and rubbings and plaster casts and dusty old runes. He has spent all his life away back in the tenth century, and now he is going farther, farther....

"Oh, I'm aweary, aweary! If anything happens to grandfather I shall soon leave this place; there will be nothing to hold me here any longer, and besides I could not bear the sight of these evidences of his gentle presence, so simple, so touching. But what a vain thing London is with all its vast ado—how little, how pitiful!

"Later.—It is all over! The curtain has fallen, and I am not crying. If I did cry it would not be from grief, but because the end was so beautiful, so glorious! It was at sunset, and the streamers of the sun were coming horizontally into the room. He awoke from a long drowsiness, and a serenity almost angelic overspread his face. I could see that he was himself once again. Death had led him back through the long years since he was a child, and he knew he was an old man and I a young woman. 'Have the boats gone yet?' he asked, meaning the herring boats that go at sunset. I looked out and told him they were at the point of going. 'Let me see them sail,' he said, so I slipped my arms about him and raised him until he was sitting up and could see down the length of the harbour and past the castle to the sea. The reflection of the sunlight was about his silvery old head, and over the damps and chills of death it made a radiance on his face like a light from heaven. There was hardly a breeze, and the boats were dropping down from their berths with their brown sails half set. 'Ah,' he said, 'it's the other way with me, Glory. I'm coming in, not going out. I've been beating to windward all my life, but I see the harbour on my lee-bow at last as plainly as I ever saw Peel, and now I'm only waiting for the top of the tide and the master of the port to run up the flag!'

"Then his head fell gently back on my arm and his lips changed colour, but his eyes did not close, and over his saintly face there passed a fleeting smile. Thus died a Christian gentleman—a simple, sunny, merry, happy, childlike creature, and of such are the kingdom of heaven.

"Glory."

Parson Quayle's Letter.

"Dear John: Before this letter reaches you, or perhaps along with it, you will receive the news that tells you what it is. I am 'in,' John; I can say no more than that. The doctor tells me it may be now or then or at any time. But I am looking for my enlargement soon, and whether it comes to-morrow sunset or with to-day's next tide I leave myself in His hands in whose hands we all are. Well has the wise man said, 'The day of our death is better than the day of our birth, so with all good will, and what legacy of strength old age has left to me, I send you my last word and message.

"My poor old daughters are sorely stricken, but Glory is still brave and true, being, as she always was, a quivering bow of steel. People tell me that the poor mother is strong in the girl, and the spirit of the mother's race; but well I know the father's stalwart soul supports her; and I pray God that when my dark hour comes her loving and courageous arms may be around me.

"That brings me to the object of my letter. This living will soon be vacant, and I am wondering who will follow in my feeble steps. It is a sweet spot, John! The old church does not look so ill when the sun shines on it, and in the summer-time this old garden is full of fruit and flowers. Did I ever tell you that Glory was born here? I never had another grandchild, and we were great comrades from the first. She was a wise and winsome little thing, and I was only an old child myself, so we had many a run and romp in these grounds together. When I try to think of the place without her it is a vain effort and a painful one; and even while she was away in your great and wicked Babylon, with its dangers and temptations, her little ghost seemed to lurk at the back of every bush and tree, and sometimes it would leap out on me and laugh.

"It is months since I saw your father, but they tell me he has lately burned his bureau, making one vast bonfire of the gatherings of twenty years. That is not such ill news either; and maybe, now the great ado that worked such woe is put by and gone, he would rejoice to see you back at home, and open his hungering arms to you.

"But my eyes ache and my pen is shaking. Farewell! Farewell! Farewell! An old man leaves you his blessing, John. God grant that in his own good time we may meet in a blessed paradise, rejoicing in his gracious mercy, and all our sins forgiven!

"Adam Quayle."

CHAPTER X

Glory's letter and its inclosure fell on John Storm like rain in the face of a man on horseback—he only whipped up and went faster.

"How can I find words," he wrote, "to express what I feel at your mournful news? Yet why mournful? His life's mission was fulfilled, his death was a peaceful victory, and we ought to rejoice that he was so easily released. I trust you will not mourn too heavily for him, or allow his death to stop your life. It would not be right. No trouble came near his stainless heart, no shadow of sin; his old age was a peaceful day which lasted until sunset. He was a creature that had no falsetto in a single fibre of his being, no shadow of affectation. He kept like this through all our complicated existence in this artificial world, absolutely unconscious of the hollowness and pretension and sham that surrounded him—tolerant, too, and kind to all. Then why mourn for him? He is gathered in—he is safe.

"His letter was touching in its artful simplicity. It was intended to ask me to apply for his living. But my duty is here, and London must make the best of me. Yet more than ever now I feel my responsibility with regard to yourself. The time is not ripe to advise you. I am on the eve of a great effort. Many things have to be tried, many things attempted. It is a gathering of manna—a little every day. To God's keeping and protection meantime I commit you. Comfort your aunts, and let me know if there is anything that can be done for them."

The ink of this letter was hardly dry when John Storm was in the middle of something else. He was in a continual fever now. Above all, his great scheme for the rescue and redemption of women and children possessed him. He called it Glory's scheme when he talked of it to himself. It might be in the teeth of nineteenth-century morality, but what matter about that? It was on the lines of Christ's teaching when he forgave the woman and shamed the hypocrites. He would borrow for it, beg for it, and there might be conditions under which he would steal for it too.

Mrs. Callender shook her head.

"I much misdoubt there'll be scandal, laddie. It's a woman's work, I'm thinking."

"'Be thou as chaste as ice,' auntie, 'as pure as snow' ... but no matter! I intend to call out the full power of a united Church into the warfare against this high wickedness. Talk of the union of Christendom! If we are in earnest about it we'll unite to protect and liberate our women."

"But where's the siller to come frae, laddie?"

"Anywhere—everywhere! Besides, I have a bank I can always draw on, auntie."

"You're no meaning the Prime Minister again, surely?"

"I mean the King of Kings. God will provide for me, in this, as in everything."

Thus his reckless enthusiasm bore down everything, and at the back of all his thoughts was the thought of Glory. He was preparing a way for her; she was coming back to a great career, a glorious mission; her bright soul would shine like a star; she would see that he had been right, and faithful, and then—then——But it was like wine coursing through his veins—he could not think of it.

Three thousand pounds had to be found to buy or build homes with, and he set out to beg for the money. His first call was at Mrs. Macrae's. Going up to the house, he met the lady's poodle in a fawn-coloured wrap coming out in charge of a footman for its daily walk round the square.

He gave the name of "Father Storm," and after some minutes of waiting he was told that the lady had a headache and was not receiving that day.

"Say the nephew of the Prime Minister wishes to see her," said John.

Before the footman had returned again there was the gentle rustle of a dress on the stairs, and the lady herself was saying: "Dear Mr. Storm, come up. My servants are real tiresome, they are always confusing names."

Time had told on her; she was looking elderly, and the wrinkles about her eyes could no longer be smoothed out. But her "front" was curled, and she was still saturated in perfume.

"I heard of your return, dear Mr. Storm," she said, in the languid voice of the great lady, but the accent of St. Louis, as she led the way to the drawing-room. "My daughter told me about it. She was always interested in your work, you know.... Oh, yes, quite well, and having a real good time in Paris. Of course, you know she has been married. A great loss to me naturally, but being God's will I felt it was my duty as a mother— —" and then a pathetic description of her maternal sentiments, consoled by the circumstance that her son-in-law belonged to "one of the best families," and that she was constantly getting newspapers from "the other side" containing full accounts of the wedding and of the dresses that were worn at it.

John twirled his hat in his hand and listened.

"And what are your dear devoted people doing down there in Soho?"

Then John told of his work for working girls, and the great lady pretended to be deeply interested. "Why, they'll soon be better than the upper classes," she said.

John thought it was not improbable, but he went on to tell of his scheme, and how small was the sum required for its execution.

"Only three thousand! That ought to be easily fixed up. Why, certainly!"

"Charity is the salt of riches, madam, and if rich people would remember that their wealth is a trust— —"

"I do—I always do. 'Lay not up for yourselves treasure on earth'—what a beautiful text *that* is!"

"I'm glad to hear you say so, madam. So many Christian people allow that God is the God of the widow and fatherless, while the gods they really worship are the gods of silver and gold."

"But I love the dear children, and I like to go to the institution to see them in their nice white pinafores making their curtsies. But what you say is real true, Mr. Storm; and since I came from Sent Louis I've seen considerable people who are that silly about cats— —" and then a long story of the folly of a lady friend who once had a pet Persian, but it died, and she wore crape for it, and you could never mention a cat in her hearing afterward.

At that moment the poodle came back from its walk, and the lady called it to her, fondled it affectionately, said it was a present from her poor dear husband, and launched into an account of her anxieties respecting it, being delicate and liable to colds, notwithstanding the trousseau (it was a lady poodle) which the fashionable dog tailor in Regent Street had provided for it.

John got up to take his leave. "May I then count on your kind support on behalf of our poor women and children of Soho?"

"Ah, of course, that matter—well, you see the Archdeacon kindly comes to talk 'City' with me—in fact, I'm expecting him to-day—and I never do anything without asking his advice, never, in my present state of health—I have a weak heart, you know," with her head aside and her saturated pocket-handkerchief at her nose. "But has the Prime Minister done anything?"

"He has advanced me two thousand pounds."

"Really?" rising and kicking back her train. "Well, as I say, we ought to fix it right away. Why not hold a meeting in my drawing-room? All denominations, you say? I don't mind—not in a cause like that," and she glanced round her room as if thinking it was always possible to disinfect it afterward.

Somebody was coughing loudly in the hall as John stepped downstairs. It was the Archdeacon coming in. "Ah," he exclaimed, with a flourish of the hand, greeting John as if they had parted yesterday and on the best of terms. Yes, there *had* been changes, and he was promoted to a sphere of higher usefulness. True, his good friends had looked for something still higher, but it was the premier archdeaconry at all events, and in the Church, as in life generally, the spirit of compromise ruled everything. He asked what John was doing, and on being told he said, with a somewhat more worldly air, "Be careful, my dear Storm, don't encourage vice. For my part, I am tired of the 'fallen sister.' To tell you the truth, I deny the name. The painted Jezebel of the Piccadilly pavement is no sister of mine."

"We don't choose our relations, Archdeacon," said John. "If God is our Father, then all men are our brothers, and all women are our sisters whether we like it or not."

"Ah! The same man still, I see. But we will not quarrel about words. Seen the dear Prime Minister lately? Not *very* lately? Ah, well"—with a superior smile—"the air of Downing Street—it's so bad for the memory, they say," and coughing loudly again, he stepped upstairs.

John Storm went home that day light-handed but with a heavy heart.

"Begging is an ill trade on a fast day, laddie," said Mrs. Callender. "Sit you down and tak' some dinner."

"How dare these people pray, 'Our Father which art in heaven?' It's blasphemy! It's deceit!"

"Aye, and they would deceive God about their dividends if he couldn't see into their safes."

"Their money is the meanest thing Heaven gives them. If I asked them for their health or their happiness, Lord God, what would they say?"

On the Sunday night following John Storm preached to an overflowing congregation from the text, "This people draweth nigh unto me with their mouth and honoureth me with their lips, but their heart is far from me."

But a few weeks afterward his face was bright and his voice was cheery, and he was writing another letter to Glory:

"In full swing at last, Glory. To carry out my new idea I had to get three thousand pounds more of my mother's money from my uncle. He gave it up cheerfully, only saying he was curious to see what approach to the Christian ideal the situation of civilization permitted. But Mrs. Callender is *dour*, and every time I spend sixpence of my own money on the Church she utters withering sarcasms about being only a 'daft auld woman hersel',' and then I have to caress and coax her.

"The newspapers were facetious about my 'Baby Houses' until they scented the Prime Minister at the back of them, and now they call them the 'Storm Shelters,' and christen my nightly processions 'The White-cross Army.' Even the Archdeacon has begun to tell the world how he 'took an interest' in me from the first and gave me my title. I met him again the other day at a rich woman's house, where we had only one little spar, and yesterday he wrote urging me to 'organize my great effort,' and have a public dinner in honour of its inauguration. I did not think God's work could be well done by people dining in herds and drinking bottles of champagne, but I showed no malice. In fact, I agreed to hold a meeting in the lady's drawing-room, to which clergymen, laymen, and members of all denominations are being invited, for this is a cause that rises above all differences of dogma, and I intend to try what can be done toward a union of Christendom on a social basis. Mrs. Callender is dour on that subject too, reminding me that where the carcass is there will the eagles be gathered together. The Archdeacon thinks we must have the meeting before the twelfth of August, or not until after the middle of September, and Mrs. Callender understands this to mean that 'the Holy Ghost always goes to sleep in the grouse season.'

"Meantime my Girls' Club goes like a forest fire. We are in our renovated clergy-house at last, and have everything comfortable. Two hundred members already, chiefly dressmakers and tailors, and girls out of the jam and match factories. The bright, merry young things, rejoicing in their brief blossoming time between girlhood and womanhood. I love to be among them and to look at their glistening eyes! Mrs. Callender blows withering blasts on this head also, saying it is no place for a 'laddie,' whereupon I lie low and think much but say nothing.

"Our great night is Sunday night after service. Yes, indeed, Sunday! That's just when the devil's houses are all open round about us, and why should God's house be shut up? It is all very well for the people who have only one Sabbath in the week to keep it wholly holy—I have seven, being a follower of Jesus, not of Moses. But the rector of the parish has begun to complain of my 'intrusion,' and to tell the Bishop I ought to be 'mended or ended.' It seems that my 'doings' are 'indecent and unnecessary,' and my sermons are 'a violation of all the sanctities, all the modesties of existence.' Poor dumb dog, teaching the Gospel of Don't! The world has never been reformed by 'resignation' to the evils of life, or converted by 'silence' either.

"How I wish you were here, in the midst of it all! And—who knows?—perhaps you will be some day yet. Do not trouble to answer this—I will write again soon, and may then have something practical to say to you. *Au revoir!*"

CHAPTER XI

On the day of the drawing-room meeting a large company gathered in the hall at Belgrave Square. Lady Robert Ure, back from the honeymoon, received the guests for her mother, whose weak heart and a headache kept her upstairs. Her husband stood aside, chewing the end of his mustache and looking through his eyeglass with a gleam of amused interest in his glittering eye. There were many ladies, all fashionably dressed, and one of them wore a seagull's wing in her hat, with part of the root left visible and painted red to show that it had been torn out of the living bird. The men were nearly all clergymen, and the cut of their cloth and the fashions of their ties indicated the various complexions of their creeds. They glanced at each other with looks of embarrassment, and Mrs. Callender, who came in like a breeze off a Scottish moor, said audibly that she had never seen "sae many craws on one tree before." The Archdeacon was there with his head up, talking loudly to Lady Robert. She stood motionless in her place, never turning her head toward John Storm, though it was plain that she was looking at him constantly. More than once he caught an expression of pain in her face, and felt pity for her as one of the brides who had acted the lie of marrying without love. But his spirits were high. He welcomed everybody, and even bantered Mrs. Callender when she told him she "objected to the hale thing," and said, "Weel, weel, wait a wee."

The Archdeacon gave the signal and led the way with Lady Robert to the drawing-room, where Mrs. Macrae, redolent of perfume, was reclining on a sofa with the "lady poodle" by her side. As soon as the company were seated the Archdeacon rose and coughed loudly.

"Ladies and gentlemen," he said, "we have no assurance of a blessing except 'Ask and ye shall receive.' Therefore, before we go further, it is our duty, as brethren of a common family in Christ, to ask the blessing of Almighty God on this enterprise."

There was a subdued rustle of drooping hats and bonnets, when suddenly a thin voice was heard to say, "Mr. Archdeacon, may I inquire first who is to ask the blessing?"

"I thought of doing so myself," said the Archdeacon with a meek smile.

"In that case, as a Unitarian, I must object to an invocation in which I do not believe."

There was a half-suppressed titter from the wall at the back, where Lord Robert Ure was standing with his face screwed up to his eyeglass.

"Well, if the name of our Lord is a stumbling block to our Unitarian, brother, no doubt the prayer in this instance would be acceptable without the customary Christian benediction."

"That's just like you," said a large man near the door, with whiskers all round his face. "You've been trimming all your life, and now you are going to trim away the name of our Lord Jesus Christ."

"If our Low-Church brother thinks he can do better——"

But John Storm intervened. He had looked icy cold, though the twitching of his lower lip showed that he was red hot within.

"Ladies and gentlemen," he said in a quavering voice, "I apologize for bringing you together. I thought if we were in earnest about the union of Christendom we might at least unite in the real contest with evil. But I find it is a dream; we have only been trifling with ourselves, and there is not one of us who wants the union of Christendom, except on the condition that his rod shall be like Aaron's rod which swallowed up all the rest. It was a mistake, and I beg your pardon."

"Yes, sir," said the Archdeacon, "it *was* a mistake; and if you had taken my advice from the first, and asked the blessing of God through good High Churchmen alone——"

"God doesn't wait for any asking," said John, now flushing up to the eyes. "He gives freely to High Churchmen, Low Churchmen, and No Churchmen alike."

"If that is your opinion, sir, you are no better than some of your friends, and for my part I will never darken your door again!"

"*Darken* is a good word for it, Archdeacon," said John, and with that the company broke up.

Mrs. Macrae looked like a thunder-cloud as John bowed to her on passing out, but Mrs. Callender cried out in a jubilant voice, "Be skipper of your ain ship, laddie!" and added (being two yards behind the Archdeacon's broad back going down the stairs), "If some folks are to be inheritors of the kingdom of heaven there'll be a michty crush at the pearly gates, I'm thinking!"

John Storm went back to Soho with a heavy heart. Going up Victoria Street he passed a crowd of ragged people who were ploughing their way through the carriages. Two constables were taking a man and woman to the police court in Rochester Row. The prisoners were Sharkey, the keeper of the gambling house, and his wife the baby-farmer.

But within a week John Storm, in greater spirits than ever, was writing to Glory again:

"The Archdeacon has deserted me, but no matter! My uncle has advanced me another thousand of my mother's money, so the crusade is *self*-supporting in one sense at all events. What a fool I am! Ask Aunt Anna her opinion of me, or say old Chalse or the village natural—but never mind! Folly and wisdom are relative terms, and I don't envy the world its narrow ideas of either. You would be amused to see how the women of the West End are taking up the movement—Lady Robert Ure among the rest! They have banded themselves into a Sisterhood, and christened our clergy-house a 'Settlement.' One of my Greek owners came in the other evening to see the alterations. His eyes glistened at the change, and he asked leave to bring a friend. I trust you are well and settling things comfortably, and that Miss Macquarrie has gone. It is raining through a colander here, but I have no time to think of depressing weather. Sometimes when I cross our great squares, where the birds sing among the yellowing leaves, my mind goes off to your sweet home in the sunshine; and when I drop into the dark alleys and lanes, where the pale-faced children play in their poverty and rags, I think of a day that is coming, and, God willing, is now so near, when a ministering angel of tenderness and strength will be passing through them like a gleam. But I am more than ever sure that you do well to avoid for the present the pompous joys of life in London, where for one happy being there are a thousand pretenders to happiness."

On the Sunday night following, Crook Lane, outside the clergy-house, was almost blocked with noisy people of both sexes. They were a detachment of the "Skeletons," and the talk among them was of the trial of the Sharkeys, which had taken place the day before. "They've 'ed six menths," said one. "And it's all along o' minjee parsons," said another; and Charlie Wilkes, who had a certain reputation for humour, did a step-dance and sang some doggerel beginning—

> *Father Storm is a werry good man,*
>
> *'E does you all the 'arm 'e can.*

Through this crowd two gentlemen pushed their way to the clergy-house, which was brilliantly lit up. One of them was the Greek owner, the other was Lord Robert Ure. Entering a large room on the ground floor, they first came upon John Storm, in cassock and biretta, standing at the door and shaking hands with everybody who came in and went out. He betrayed no surprise, but greeted them respectfully and then passed them on. Every moment of his time was occupied. The room was full of the young girls of the district, with here and there a Sister out of another world entirely. Some were reading, some conversing, some laughing, some playing a piano, and some singing. Their voices filled the air like the chirping of birds, and their faces were bright and happy. "Good-evening, Father," they said on entering, and "Good-night, Father," as they went away.

The two men stood some minutes and looked round the room. It was observed that Lord Robert did not remove his hat. He kept chewing the end of a broken cigarette, whereof the other end hung down his chin. One of the Sisters heard him say, "It will do with a little alteration, I think." Then he went off alone, and the Greek owner stepped up to John Storm.

It was not at first that John could attend to him, and when he was able to do so he began to rattle on about his own affairs. "See," he said with a delighted smile and a wave of the arm, "see how crowded we are! We'll have to think of taking in the next door soon."

"Father Storm," said the Greek, "I have something serious to say, though the official notification will of course reach you by another channel."

John's face darkened as a ripe cornfield does when the sun dies away from it.

"I am sorry to tell you that the trustees, having had a favourable offer for this property——"

"Well?" His great staring eyes had stopped the man.

"——have decided to sell."

"*Sell*? Did you say se——? To whom? What?"

"To tell you the truth, to the syndicate of a music hall."

John staggered back, breathing audibly. "Now if a man had to believe that—Do you know if I thought such a thing *could* happen——"

"I'm sorry you take the matter so seriously, Father Storm. It's true you've spent money on the property, but, believe me, the trustees will derive no profit——"

"Profit? Money? Do you suppose I'm thinking of that, and not of the desecration, the outrage, the horror? But who are they? Is that man—Lord——"

The Greek had nodded his head, and John flung open the door. "Out of this! Out of it, you Judas!" And almost before the Greek had crossed the threshold the door was banged at his back.

The incident had been observed, and there was dead silence in the club-room, but John only cried, "Let's sing something, girls," and when a Sister struck up his favourite Nazareth there was no voice so loud as his.

But he had realized everything. "Gloria" was coming back, and the work of months was overthrown!

When he was going home groups of the girls were talking in whispers in the hall, and Mrs. Pincher, who was wiping her eyes at the door, said, "I wonder you don't drown yourself—I do!"

At the corner of the lane Mr. Jupe was waiting for him to beg his pardon and to ask his advice. What he had said of Mrs. Jupe had turned out to be true. The Sharkeys had "split" on her and she had been arrested. "It was all in the evenin' pipers last night," the weak creature whimpered, "and to-day my manager told me I 'ad best look out for another place. Oh, my poor Lidjer! What am I to do?"

"Do? Cut her off like a rotten bough!" said John scornfully, and with that he strode down the street. The human sea roared around him, and he felt as if he wanted to fling himself into the midst of it and be swallowed up.

On reaching Victoria Square he told Mrs. Callender the news—flung it out at her with a sort of triumphant shout. His church had been sold over his head, and being only "Chaplain to the Greek-Turks," he was to be turned into the streets. Then he laughed wildly, and by some devilish impulse began to abuse Glory. "The next chaplain is to be a girl," he cried, "one of those creatures who throw kisses at gaping crowds and sweep curtsies for their dirty crusts."

But all at once he turned white as a ghost and sat down trembling. Mrs. Callender's face was twitching, and to prevent herself from crying she burst into scorching satire. "There!" she said, sitting in her rocking-chair and rocking herself furiously, "I ken'd weel what it would come til! Adversity mak's a man wise, they say, if it doesna mak' him rich. But it's the Prime Minister I blame for this. The auld dolt! he must be fallen to his dotage. It's enough to mak' a reasonable body go out of her mind to think of sic wise asses. I told you what to expect, but you were always miscalling me for a suspicious auld woman. Oh, it's a thing ye'd no suspect; but Jane Callender is only a daft auld fool, ye see, and doesna ken what she's saying!"

But at the next moment she had jumped up and flung her arms about John's neck, and was crying over him like a girl. "Oh, my son! my ain son! And is it for me to fling out at ye? Aye, aye, it's a heartless world, laddie!"

He kissed the old woman, and then she tried to coax him to eat. "Come, come, a wee bittie, just a wee bittie. We must eat our supper anyway."

"God seems dead and heaven a long way off!" he murmured.

"And a drap o' whisky will do no harm—a wee drappie."

"There's only one thing clear—God sees I'm unfit for the work, so he has taken it away from me."

She turned aside from the table, and the supper was left untouched.

The first post next morning brought a letter from Glory.

"The Garden House,

"Clement's Inn, W. C.

"Forgive me! I have returned to town! I couldn't help it, I couldn't, I couldn't! London dragged me back. What was I to do after everything was settled and the aunties provided for?—assist in a dame's school and wage war with pothooks and hangers? Oh! I was dying of weariness—dying, dying, dying!

"And then they made me such tempting offers. Not the music hall—don't think that. I dare say you were quite right there. No, but the theatre, the regular theatre! Mr. Drake has bought some broken-down old place, and is to turn it into a beautiful theatre expressly for me. I am to play Juliet. Only think—Juliet!—and in my own theatre! Already I feel like a liberated slave who has crossed her Red Sea.

"And don't think a woman's mourning is like the silly old laws which lasted but three days. *He* is buried in my heart, not in the earth, and I shall love him and revere him always! And then didn't you tell me yourself it would not be right to allow his death to stop my life?

"Write and say you forgive me, John. Reply by return, and make yourself your own postman—registered. You'll find me here at Rosa's. Come, come, come! I'll never forgive you if you don't come soon—never, never!

"Glory."

CHAPTER XII

A fortnight had passed, and John Storm had not yet visited Glory. Nevertheless, he had heard of her from day to day through the medium of the newspapers. Every morning he had glanced down the black columns for the name that stood out from them as if its letters had been printed in blood. The reports had been many and mysterious. First, the brilliant young artiste, who had made such an extraordinary impression some months before, had returned to London and would shortly resume the promising career which had been interrupted by illness and family bereavement. Next, the forthcoming appearance would be on the regular stage, and in a Shakespearian character, which was always understood to be a crucial test of histrionic genius. Then, the revival of Romeo and Juliet, which had formerly been in contemplation, would probably give way to the still more ambitious project of an entirely new production by a well-known Scandinavian author, with a part peculiarly fitted to the personality and talents of the *débutante*. Finally, a syndicate was about to be formed for the purchase of some old property, with a view to its reconstruction as a theatre, in the interests of the new play and the new player.

John Storm laughed bitterly. He told himself that Glory was unworthy of the least of his thoughts. It was his duty to go on with his work and think of her no more.

He had received his official notice to quit. The church was to be given up in a month, the clergy-house in two months, and he believed himself to be immersed in preparations for the rehousing of the club and home. Twenty young mothers and their children now lived in the upper rooms, under obedience to the Sisterhood, but Polly's boy had remained with Mrs. Pincher. From time to time he had seen the little one tethered to a chair by a scarf about its waist, creeping by the wall to the door, and there gazing out on the world with looks of intelligence, and babbling to it in various inarticulate noises. "Boo-loo! Lal-la! Mum-um!" The little dark face had the eyes of its mother, but it represented Glory for all that. John Storm loved to see it. He felt that he could never part with it, and that if Lord Robert Ure himself came and asked for it he would bundle him out of doors.

But a carriage drew up at Mrs. Callender's one morning, and Lady Robert Ure stepped out. Her pale and patient face had the feeble and nervous smile of the humiliated and unloved.

"Mr. Storm," she said in her gentle voice, "I have come on a delicate errand. I can not delay any longer a duty I ought to have discharged before."

It was about Polly's baby. She had heard of what had happened at the hospital; and the newspapers which had followed her to Paris, with reports of her wedding, had contained reports of the girl's death also. Since her return she had inquired about the child, and discovered that it had been rescued by him and was now in careful keeping.

"But it is for me to look after it, Mr. Storm, and I beg of you to give it up to me. Something tells me that God will never give me children of my own, so I shall be doing no harm to any one, and my husband need never know whose child it is I adopt. I promise you to be good to it. It shall never leave me. And if it should live to be a man, and grow to love me, that will help me to forget the past and to forgive myself for my own share in it. Oh, it is little I can do for the poor girl who is gone—for, after all, she loved him and I took him from her. But this is my duty, Mr. Storm, and I can not sleep at night or rest in the day until it is begun."

"I don't know if it is your duty, dear lady, but if you wish for the child it is your right," said John Storm, and they got into the carriage and drove to Soho.

"Boo-loo! Lal-la! Mum-um!" The child was tethered to the chair as usual and talking to the world according to its wont. When it was gone and the women on the doorsteps could see no more of the fine carriage of the great lady who had brought the odour of perfume and the rustle of silk into the dingy court, and Mrs. Pincher had turned back to the house with red eyes and her widow's cap awry, John Storm told himself that everything was for the best. The last link with Glory was broken! Thank God for that! He might go on with his work now and need think of her no more!

That day he called at Clement's Inn.

The Garden House was a pleasant dwelling, fronting on two of its sides to the garden of the ancient Inn of Chancery, and cosily furnished with many curtains and rugs. The Cockney maid who answered the door was familiar in a moment, and during the short passage from the hall to the floor above she communicated many things. Her name was Liza; she had heard him preach; he had made her cry; "Miss Gloria" had known her former mistress, and Mr. Drake had got her the present place.

There was a sound of laughter from the drawing-room. It was Glory's voice. When the door opened she was standing in the middle of the floor in a black dress and with a pale face, but her eyes were bright and she was laughing merrily. She stopped when John Storm entered and looked confused and ashamed. Drake, who was lounging on the couch, rose and bowed to him, and Miss Macquarrie, who was correcting long slips of printer's proofs at a desk by the window, came forward and welcomed him. Glory held his hand with her long hand-clasp and looked steadfastly into his eyes. His face twitched and her own blushed deeply, and then she talked in a nervous and jerky way, reproaching him for his neglect of her.

"I have been busy," he began, and then stopped with a sense of hypocrisy. "I mean worried and tormented," and then stopped again, for Drake had dropped his head.

She laughed, though there was nothing to laugh at, and proposed tea, rattling along in broken sentences that were spoken with a tremulous trill, which had a suggestion of tears behind it. "Shall I ring for tea, Rosa? Oh, you *have* rung for tea! Ah, here it comes!—Thank you, Liza. Set it here," seating herself. "Now who says the 'girl'? Remember?" and then more laughter.

At that moment there was another arrival. It was Lord Robert Ure. He kissed Rosa's hand, smiled on Glory, saluted Drake familiarly, and then settled himself on a low stool by the tea-table, pulled up the knees of his trousers, relaxed the congested muscles of one half of his face, and let fall his eyeglass.

Drake was handing out the cups as Glory filled them. He was looking at her attentively, vexed at the change in her manner since John Storm entered. When he returned to his seat on the sofa he began to twitch the ear of her pug, which lay coiled up asleep beside him, calling it an ugly little pestilence, and wondering why she carried it about with her. Glory protested that it was an angel of a dog, whereupon he supposed it was now dreaming of paradise—listen!—and then there were audible snores in the silence, and everybody laughed, and Glory screamed.

"I declare, on my honour, my dear," said Drake with a mischievous look at John, "the creature is uglier than the beast that did the business on the day we eloped."

"Eloped!" cried Rosa and Lord Robert together.

"Why, did you never hear that Glory eloped with me?"

Glory was trying to drown his voice with hollow laughter.

"She was seven and I was six and a half, and she had proposed to me in the orchard the day before!"

"Anybody have more tea? No? Some sally-lunn, perhaps?" and then more laughter.

"Hold your tongue, Glory! Nobody wants your tea! Let us hear the story," said Rosa.

"Why, yes, certainly," said Lord Robert, and everybody laughed again.

"She was all for travel and triumphal processions in those days— —"

Glory stopped her ears and began to sing:

Willy, Willy Wilkin,

Kissed the maid a-milkin'!

Fa, la la!

"There were so many things people could do if they wouldn't waste so much time working— —"

Willy, Willy Wilkin

Kissed the maid— —

"Glory, if you don't be quiet we'll turn you out!" and Rosa got up and nourished her proofs.

"I had brought my dog, and when I called her a— —"

But Glory had leaped to her feet and fled from the room. Drake had leaped up also, and now, putting his back against the door, he raised his voice and went on with his story.

"Somebody saved us, though, and she lay in his arms and kissed him all the way home again."

Glory was strumming on the door and singing to drown his voice. When the story was ended and she was allowed to come back she was panting and gasping with laughter, but there were tears in her eyes for all that, and Lord Robert was saying, with a sidelong look toward John Storm, "Really, this ought to be a scene in the new Sigurdsen, don't you know!"

John had retired within himself during this nonsense. He had been feeling an intense hatred of the two men, and was looking as gloomy as deep water. "All acting, sheer acting," he thought, and then he told himself that Glory was only worthy of his contempt. What could attract her in the society of such men? Only their wealth, and their social station. Their intellectual and moral atmosphere must weary and revolt her.

Rosa had to go to her newspaper office, and Drake saw her to the door. John rose at the same time, and Glory said, "Going already?" but she did not try to detain him. She would see him again; she had much to say to him.

"I suppose you were surprised to hear that I had returned to London?" she said, looking up at his knitted brows.

He did not answer immediately, and Lord Robert, who was leaning against the chimney-piece, said in his cold drawl, "Your friend ought to be happy that you have returned to London, seems to me, my dear, instead of wasting your life in that wilderness."

John drew himself up. "It's not London I object to," he said; "that was inevitable, I dare say."

"What then?"

"The profession she has come back to follow."

"Why, what's amiss with the profession?" said Lord Robert, and Drake, who returned to the room at the moment, said: "Yes, what's amiss with it? Some of the best men in the world have belonged to it, I think."

"Tell me the name of one of them, since the world began, who ever lived an active Christian life."

Lord Robert made a kink of laughter, and, turning to the window, began to play a tune with his finger tips on the glass of a pane. Drake struggled to keep a straight face, and answered, "It is not their rôle, sir."

"Very well, if that's too much to ask, tell me how many of them have done anything in real life, anything for the world, for humanity—anything whatever, I don't care what it is."

"You are unreasonable, sir," said Drake, "and such objections could as properly apply to the professions of the painter and the musician. These are the children of joy. Their first function is to amuse. And surely amusement has its place in real life, as you say."

"On the contrary," said John, following his own thought, for he had not listened, "how many of them have lived lives of reckless abandonment, self-indulgence, and even scandalous license!"

"Those are abuses that apply equally to other professions, sir. Even the Church is not free from them. But in the view of reasonable beings one clergyman of evil life—nay, one hundred—would not make the profession of the clergy bad."

"A profession," said John, "which appeals above all to the senses, and lives on the emotions, and fosters jealousy and vanity and backbiting, and develops duplicity, and exists on lies, and does nothing to encourage self-sacrifice or to help suffering humanity, is a bad profession and a sinful one!"

"If a profession is sinful," said Drake, "in proportion as it appeals to the senses, and lives on the emotions, and develops duplicity, then the profession of the Church is the most sinful in the world, for it offers the greatest temptations to lying, and produces the worst hypocrites and impostors!"

"That," said John, with eyes flashing and passion vibrating in his voice—"that, sir, is the great Liar's everlasting lie—and you know it!"

Glory was between them with uplifted hands. "Peace, peace! Blessed is the peacemaker! But tea! Will nobody take more tea? Oh, dear! oh, dear! Why can't we have tea over again?"

"I know what you mean, sir," said Drake. "You mean that I have brought Glory back to a life of danger and vanity, and sloth and sensuality. Very well. I deny your definition. But call it what you will, I have brought her back to the only life her talents are fit for, and if that's all——"

"Would you have done the same for your own sister?"

"How dare you introduce my sister's name in this connection?"

"And how dare you resent it? What's good for one woman is good for another."

Glory was turning aside, and Drake was looking ashamed. "Of course—naturally—all I meant," he faltered—"if a girl has to earn her living, whatever her talents, her genius—that is one thing. But the upper classes, I mean the leisured classes——"

"Damn the leisured classes, sir!" said John, and in the silence that followed the men looked round, but Glory was gone from the room.

Lord Robert, who had been whistling at the window, said to Drake in a cynical undertone: "The man is hipped and sore. He has lost his challenge, and we ought to make allowances for him, don't you know."

Drake tried to laugh. "I'm willing to make allowances," he said lightly; "but when a man talks to me as if—as if I meant to——" but the light tone broke down, and he faced round upon John and burst out passionately: "What right have you to talk to me like this? What is there in my character, in my life, that justifies it? What woman's honour have I betrayed? What have I done that is unworthy of the character of an English gentleman?"

John took a stride forward and came face to face and eye to eye with him. "What have you done?" he said. "You have used a woman as your decoy to win your challenge, as you say, and you have struck me in the face with the hand of the woman I love! That's what you've done, sir, and if it's worthy of the character of an English gentleman, then God help England!"

Drake put his hand to his head and his flushed face turned pale. But Lord Robert Ure stepped forward and said with a smile: "Well, and if you've lost your church so much the better. You are only an outsider in the ecclesiastical stud anyway. Who wants you? Your rector doesn't want you; your Bishop doesn't want you. Nobody wants you, if you ask me."

"I don't ask you, Lord Robert," said John. "But there's somebody who does want me for all that. Shall I tell you who it is? It's the poor and helpless girl who has been deceived by the base and selfish man, and then left to fight the battle of life alone, or to die by suicide and go shuddering down to hell! That's who wants me, and, God willing, I mean to stand by her."

"Damme, sir, if you mean *me*, let me tell you what *you* are," said Lord Robert, screwing up his eyeglass. "You"—shaking his head right and left—"you are a man who takes delicately nurtured ladies out of sheltered homes and sends them into holes and hovels in search of abandoned women and their misbegotten children! Why"—turning to Drake-"what do you think has happened? My wife has fallen under this gentleman's influence—the poor simpleton!—and not one hour before I left my house she brought home a child which he had given her to adopt. Think of it!—out of the shambles of Soho, and God knows whose brat and bastard!"

The words were hardly out of the man's mouth when John Storm had taken him by both shoulders. "God *does* know," he said, "and so do I! Shall I tell you whose child that is? Shall I? It's yours!" The man saw it coming and turned white as a ghost. "Yours! and your wife has taken up the burden of your sin and shame, for she's a good woman, and you are not fit to live on the earth she walks upon!"

He left the two men speechless and went heavily down the stairs. Glory was waiting for him at the door. Her eyes were glistening after recent tears.

"You will come no more?" she said. She could read him like a book. "I can see that you intend to come no more."

He did not deny it, and after a moment she opened the door and he passed out with a look of utter weariness. Then she went back to her room and flung herself on the bed, face downward.

The men in the drawing-room were beginning to recover themselves. Lord Robert was humming a tune, Drake pacing to and fro.

"Buying up his church to make a theatre for Glory was the very refinement of cruelty!" said Drake. "Good heavens! what possessed me?"

"Original sin, dear boy!" said Lord Robert, with a curl of the lip.

"Original? A bad plagiarism, you mean!"

"Very well. If *I* helped you to do it, shall I help you to give it up? Withdraw the prospectus and return the deposits on shares—the dear Archdeacon's among the rest."

Drake took up his hat and left the house. Lord Robert followed him presently. Then the drawing-room was empty, and the hollow sound of sobbing came down to it from the bedroom above.

Father Storm read prayers in church that night with a hard and absent heart. A terrible impulse of hate had taken hold of him. He hated Drake, he hated Glory, he hated himself most of all, and felt as if seven devils had taken possession of him, and he was a hypocrite, and might fall dead at the altar.

"But what a fate the Almighty has saved me from!" he thought. Glory would have been a drag on his work for life. He must forget her. She was only worthy of his contempt. Yet he could not help but remember how beautiful she had looked in her mourning dress, with that pure pale face and its signs of suffering! Or how charming she had seemed to him even in the midst of all that deception! Or how she had held him as by a spell!

Going home he came upon a group of men in the Court. One of them planted himself full in front and said with an insolent swagger: "Me and my mytes thinks there's too many parsons abart 'ere. What do you think, sir?"

"I think there are more gamblers and thieves, my lad," he answered, and at the next instant the man had struck him in the face. He closed with the ruffian, grappled him by the throat, and flung him on his back. One moment he held him there, writhing and gasping, then he said, "Get up, and get off, and let me see no more of you!"

"No, sir, not this time," said a voice above his back. The crowd had melted away and a policeman stood beside them. "I've been waiting for this one for weeks, Father," he said, and he marched the man to jail.

It was Charlie Wilkes. At the trial of Mrs. Jupe that morning, Aggie, being a witness, had been required to mention his name. It was all in the evening papers, and he had been dismissed from his time-keeping at the foundry.

CHAPTER XIII

A week passed. Breakfast was over at Victoria Square, and John Storm was glancing at the pages of a weekly paper. "Listen!" he cried, and then read aloud in a light tone of mock bravery which broke down at length into a husky gurgle:

"'The sympathy which has lately been evoked by the announcement that a proprietary church in Soho has been sold for secular uses, is creditable to public sentiment— —'"

"Think of that, now!" interrupted Mrs. Callender.

"'— —and no doubt the whole community will agree to hope that Father Storm will recover from the irritation natural to his eviction— —'"

"Aye, we can all get over another body's disappointment, laddie."

"'But there is a danger that in this instance the altruism of the time may develop a sentimentality not entirely good for public morals— —'"

"When the ox is down there are lots of butchers, ye ken!"

"'With the uses to which the fabric is to be converted, it is no part of our purpose to deal, further than to warn the public not to lend an ear to the all too prurient purity of the amateur moralist; but considering the character of the work now carried on in Soho, no doubt with the best intentions— —'"

"Aye, aye, it's easy to steal the goose and give the giblets in alms."

"'— —it behooves us to consider if the community is not to be congratulated on its speedy and effectual ending. Father Storm is a young man of some talents and social position, but without any special experience or knowledge of the world—in fact a weak, oversanguine, and rather foolish fanatic— —'"

"Oh, aye, he's down; down with him!"

"'— —and therefore it is monstrous that he should be allowed to subvert the order of social life or disturb the broad grounds of the reasonable and the practical— —'"

"Never mind. High winds only blaw on high hills, laddie!"

"'——As for the "fallen sister" whom he has taken under his special care, we confess to a feeling that too much sympathy has been wasted on her already. Her feet take hold of hell, her house is the way of the grave, going down to the chamber of death——'"

Mrs. Callender leaped to her feet. "That's the 'deacon-man; I ken the cloven hoof!"

John Storm had flung the paper away. "What a cowardly world it is!" he said. "But God wins in the end, and by God he shall!"

"Tut, man! don't tak' on like that. You can't climb the Alps on roller-skates, you see! But as for the Archdeacon, pooh! I'm no windy aboot your 'Sisters' and 'Settlements' and sic like, but if there had been society papers in the Lord's time, Simon the Pharisee would have been a namby-pamby critic compared to some of them."

A moment afterward she was looking out of the window and holding up both hands. "My gracious! It's himsel'! It's the Prime Minister!"

A gaunt old gentleman with a meagre mustache, wearing a broad-brimmed hat and unfashionable black clothes, was stepping up to the door.

"Yes, it's my uncle!" said John, and the old lady fled out of the room to change her cap.

"I have heard what has happened, John, so I have come to see you," said the Prime Minister.

Was he thinking of the money? John felt uneasy and ashamed.

"I'm sorry, my boy, very sorry!"

"Thank you, uncle."

"But it all comes, you see, of the ridiculous idea that we are a Christian nation! Such a thing couldn't have occurred at the shrine of a pagan god!"

"It was only a proprietary church, uncle. I was much to blame."

"I do not deny that you have acted unwisely, but what difference does that make, my boy? To sell a church seems like the climax of irreverence; but they are doing as bad every day. If you want to see what times the Church has fallen on, look at the advertisements in your religious papers—your Benefice and Church Patronage Gazette, and so forth. A traffic, John, a slave traffic, worse than anything in Africa, where they sell bodies, not souls!"

"It is a crime which cries to the avenging anger of Heaven," said John; "but it is the Establishment that is to blame, not the Church, uncle."

"We are a nation of money-lenders, my boy, and the Church is the worst usurer of them all, with its learned divines in scarlet hoods, who hold shares in music halls, and its Fathers in God living at ease and leasing out public-houses. *You* have been lending money on usury too, and on a bad security. What are you going to do now?"

"Go on with my work, uncle, and do two hours where I did one before."

"And get yourself kicked where you got yourself kicked before!"

"Why not? If God puts ten pounds on a man, he gives him strength to bear twenty."

"John, John, I am feeling rather sore, and I can't bear much more of it. I'm growing old, and my life is rather lonely too. Except your father, you are my only kinsman now, and it seems as if our old family must die with you. But come, my boy, come, throw up all this sorry masquerade. Isn't there a woman in the world who can help me to persuade you? I don't care who she is, or what, or where she comes from."

John had coloured to the eyes, and was stammering something about the true priest cut off from earthly marriage, therefore free to commit himself completely to his work, when Mrs. Callender came back, spruce and smart, with many smiles and curtsies. The Prime Minister greeted her with the same old-fashioned courtesy, and they cooed away like two old doves, until a splendid equipage drove up to the door, and the plain old gentleman drove away in it.

"Wasn't he nice with me? wasn't he, now?" the old lady kept saying, and John being silent—"Tut! you young men are just puir loblollyboys with a leddy when the auld ones come."

Going to Soho that day John Storm felt a sudden thrill at seeing on the street in front of him, walking in the same direction, an elderly figure in cassock and cord. It was the Father Superior of the Brotherhood. John overtook him and greeted him.

"Ah, I was on my way to see you, my son."

"Then you have heard what has happened?"

"Yes, Satan's shafts fly fast." Then taking John's arm as they walked, "Earthly blows are but reminders of Him, my son, like the hair shirt of the monk, and this trouble of yours is God's reminder of your broken obedience. What did I tell you when you left us—that you would come back within a year? And you will! Leave the world, my son. It treats you badly. The human spirit reigns over it, and even the Church is a Christian society out of the sphere and guidance of the Divine Spirit. Leave it and return to your unfinished vows."

John shook his head and took the Father into the clergy-house, where the girls were gathering for the evening. "How can I leave the world, Father, when there's work like this to do? Society presents to a large proportion of these bright creatures the alternative, 'Sell yourself or starve.' But God says, 'Live, work, and love.' Therefore society is doomed, and that dead man's sepulchre, the Establishment, is doomed, but the Church will live, and become the corner-stone of the new order, and stand between woman and the world, as it stood of old between the poor and the rich."

The Father preached for John that night, taking for his text "The flesh lusteth against the Spirit, and the Spirit against the flesh." And on parting from him at the door of the sacristy he said: "Religious work can only be good, my son, if it concerns itself first of all with the salvation of souls. Now what if it pleased God to remove you from all this—to call you to a work of intercession—say, to the mission field?"

John's face turned pale. "There can be no need to fly," he said, with a frightened look. "Surely London is a mission field wide enough for any man."

"Yet who knows? Perhaps for your own soul's sake, lest vanity should take hold of you, or the love of fame, or—or any of the snares of Satan! But good-bye, and God be with you!"

When John Storm reached home he found a letter awaiting him. It was from Glory:

"Are you dead and buried? If so, send me word, that I may compose your epitaph. 'Here lies—*Lies* is good, for though you didn't promise to come back you ought to have done so; therefore it comes to the same thing in the end. You must not think too ill of Mr. Drake. I call him the milk of human kindness, and his friend Lord Robert the oil thereof—I mean the oil of vitriol. But his temper is like the Caspian Sea, having neither ebb nor flow, while yours is like the Bay of Biscay—oh, so I can't expect you to agree. As for poor me, I may be guilty of all the seven deadly sins, but I can't see why I should be boycotted on that account. There is something I didn't know when you were here, and I want to explain about it. Therefore come 'right away' (Lord Bob, Americanized). Being slow to anger and plenteous in mercy, I will forgive you if you come soon. If you don't, I'll—I'll go on the bike—feminine equivalent to the drink. To tell you the truth, I've done so already, having been careering round the gardens of the Inn during the early hours of morning, clad in Rosa's 'bloomers,' in which I make a picture and a sensation at the same time, she being several sizes larger round the hips, and fearfully and wonderfully made. If that doesn't fetch you I'll go in for boxing next, and in a pair of four-ounce gloves I'll cut a *striking* figure, I can tell you.

"But, John Storm, have you cast me off entirely? Do you intend to abandon me? Do you think there is no salvation left for me? And are you going to let me sink in all this mire without stretching out a hand to help me? Oh, dear! oh, dear! I don't know what has come over the silly old world since I came back to London. Think it must be teething, judging by the sharpness of its bite, and feel as if I should like to give it a dose of syrup of squills."

As John read the letter his eyelids quivered and his mouth relaxed. Then he glanced at it again, and his face clouded.

"I can not leave her entirely to the mercy of men like these," he thought.

This innocent daring, this babelike ripping up of serviceable conventions—God knows what advantage such men might take of it. He must see her once again, to warn, to counsel her. It was his duty—he must not shrink from it.

It had been a day of painful impressions to Glory. Early in the morning Lord Robert had called to take her to the "reading" of the new play. It took place in the saloon of an unoccupied Strand theatre, of which the stage also had been engaged for rehearsal. The company were gathered there, and, being more or less experienced actors and actresses, they received her with looks of courteous indulgence, as one whose leading place must be due to other things than talent. This stung her; she felt her position to be a false one, and was vexed that she had permitted Lord Robert to call for her. But her humiliation had yet hardly begun.

While they stood waiting for the manager, who was late, a gorgeous person with a waxed mustache and in a fur-lined coat, redolent of the mixed odour of perfume and stale tobacco, forced his way up to her and offered his card. She knew the man in a moment.

"I'm Josephs," he said in a confidential undertone, "and if there's anything I can do for you—acting management—anything—it vill give me pleesure."

Glory flushed up and said, "But you don't seem to remember, sir, that we have met before."

The man smiled blandly. "Oh, yes. I've kept track of you ever since and know all about you. You hadn't made your appearance then, and naturally I couldn't do much. But now—*now* if you vill give me de pleesure——"

"Then an agent is one who can do nothing for you when you want help, but when you don't want it——"

The man laughed to carry off his audacity. "Veil, you know vhat they say of us—agent from *agere*, 'to do,' and we're always 'doing.' Ha, ha! But if you are villing to let bygones be bygones, I am, and velcome."

Glory's face was crimson. "Will somebody go for the stage doorkeeper?" she said, and one of the company went out on that errand. Then, raising her voice so that everybody listened, she said: "Mr. Josephs, when I was quite unknown, and trying to get on, and finding it very hard, as we all do, you played me the cruellest trick a man ever played on a woman. I don't owe you any grudge, but, for the sake of every poor girl who is struggling to live in London, I am going to turn you out of the house."

"Eh? Vhat?"

The stage doorkeeper had entered. "Porter, do you see this gentleman? He is never to come into this theatre again as long as we are here, and if he tries to force his way in you are to call a policeman and have him bundled back into the street!"

"Daddle doo," and the waxed mustache over the grinning mouth seemed to cut the face across.

When Josephs had gone Glory could see that the looks of indulgence on the faces of the company had gone also. "She'll do!" said one. "She's got the stuff in her!" said another, but Glory herself was now quaking with fear, and her troubles were not yet ended.

A little stout gentleman entered hurriedly with a roll of papers in his hand. He stepped up to Lord Robert, apologized for being late, and mopped his bald crown and red face. It was Sefton.

"This is to be our manager," said Lord Robert, and Mr. Sefton bobbed his head, winked with both eyes, and said, "Charmed, I'm sure—charmed!"

Glory could have sunk into the earth for shame, but in a moment she had realized the crushing truth that when a woman has been insulted in the deepest place—in her honour—the best she can do is to say nothing about it.

The company seated themselves around the saloon, and the reading began. First came the list of characters, with the names of the cast. Glory's name and character came last, and her nerves throbbed with sudden pain when the manager read, "and *Gloria*—Miss Glory Quayle."

There was a confused murmur, and then the company composed themselves to listen. It was Gloria's play. She was rather scandalous. After the first act Glory thought it was going to be the story of Nell Gwynne in modern life; after the second, of Lady Hamilton; and after the third, in which the woman wrecks and ruins the first man in the country, she knew it was only another version of the Harlot's Progress, and must end as that had ended.

The actors were watching their own parts, and pointing and punctuating with significant looks the places where the chances came, but Glory was overwhelmed with confusion. How was she to play this evil woman? The poison went to the bone, and to get into the skin of such a creature a good woman would have to dispossess herself of her very soul. The reading ended, every member of the company congratulated some other member on the other's opportunities, and Sefton came up to Glory to ask if she did not find the play strong and the part magnificent.

"Yes," she said; "but only a bad woman could play that part properly."

"*You'll* do it, my dear, you'll do it on your own!" he answered gaily, and she went home perplexed, depressed, beaten down, and ashamed.

A newspaper had been left at the door. It was a second-rate theatrical journal, still damp from the press. The handwriting on the wrapper was that of Josephs, and there was a paragraph marked in blue pencil. It pretended to be a record of her short career, and everything was in it—the programme selling, the dressing, the foreign clubs—all the refuse of her former existence, set in a sinister light and leaving the impression of an abject up-bringing, as of one who had been *in* the streets if not on them.

Well, she had chosen her life and must take it at its own price. But, oh, the cruelty of the world to a woman, when her very success could be her shame! She felt that the past had gripped her again—the pitiless past—she could never drag herself out of the mire.

That night she wrote to John Storm, and next morning before Rosa had risen—her duties kept her up late—she heard a voice downstairs. Her dog also heard it and began to bark. At the next moment John was in the room and she was laughing up into his splendid black eyes, for he had caught her down at the sofa holding the pug's nose and trying to listen.

"Is it you? It's so good of you to come early! But this, dog"—breaking into the Manx dialect—"she's ter'ble, just ter'ble!" Then rising and looking serious: "I wished to tell you that I knew nothing about the church, nothing whatever. If I'd had the least idea... but they told me nothing—it was very wrong—nothing. And the first thing I knew was when I saw it in all the newspapers."

He was leaning on the end of the mantelpiece. "If they deceived you like that, how can you go on with them?"

"You mean" (she was leaning on the other end, and speaking falteringly), "you mean that I ought to give it all up. But it's too late for that now. It was too late when I came to know. Besides, it would do no good; you would be in the same position still, and as for me—well, somebody else would have the theatre, so where's the use?"

"I was thinking of the future, Glory, not the past. People who deceive us once are capable of doing so again."

"True—that's true—only—only——"

She was breaking down, and he turned his eyes away from her, saying, "Well, it's all over now, and there's no help for it."

"No, there's no help for it."

He tried to think what he had come to say, but do what he would he could not remember. The moment he looked at her the thread of his thoughts was lost, and the fragrance of her presence, so sweet, so close, made him feel as if he wanted to touch her. There was an awkward silence, and then he fidgeted with his hat and moved.

"Are you going so soon?"

"I'm busy, and——"

"Yes, you must be busy now."

"And then why—why should we prolong a painful interview, Glory?"

She shot up a look under her eyebrows. His eyes had a harassed expression, but there was a gleam in them that set her heart beating.

"Is it so painful? Is it?"

"Glory, I meant to tell you I could not come again."

"No! You're not so busy as all that, are you? Surely" (the Manx again, only she seemed to be breathless now)—"surely you're not so ter'ble busy but you can just put a sight on a girl now and again for all?"

He made a gesture with his hand. "It disturbs, it distracts——"

"Oh, is that all? Then," with a forced laugh, "I'll come to see you instead. Yes, I will, though."

"No, you mustn't do that, Glory. It would only torment——"

"Torment! Gough bless me! Why torment?" and a fugitive flame shot up at him.

"Because"—he stammered, and she could see that his lips quivered; then calmly, very calmly, pronouncing the words slowly, and in a voice as cold as ice—"because I love you!"

"You!"

"Didn't you know that?" His voice was guttural. "Haven't you known it all along? What's the use of pretending? You've dragged it out of me. Was that only to show your power over me?"

"Oh!"

She had heard what her heart wanted to hear, and not for worlds would she have missed hearing it, yet she was afraid, and trembling all over.

"We two are of different natures, Glory, that's the trouble between us—now, and always has been. We have nothing in common, absolutely nothing. You have chosen your path in life, and it is not my path. I have chosen mine, and it is not yours. Your friends are not my friends. We are two different beings altogether, and yet—and yet I love you! And that's why I can not come again."

It was sweet, but it was terrible. So different from what she had dreamed of: "I love you!—you are my soul!—I can not live without you!" Yet he was right. She had slain his love before it was born to her—it was born dead. In an unsteady voice, which had suddenly become husky, she said:

"No doubt you are right. I must leave you to judge. Perhaps you have thought it all out."

"Don't suppose it will be easy for me, Glory. I've suffered a good deal, and I dare say I shall suffer more yet. If so, I'll bear it. But for the sake of my work——"

"Ah!—But of course I can't expect—Naturally you love your work also——"

"I *do* love my work also, and therefore it's no use trifling. 'If thine eye offend—'"

She was stung. "Well, since there's no help for it, I suppose we must shake hands and part."

Not until then—not until he had pronounced his doom and she had accepted it did he realize how beautiful she seemed to him. He felt as if something in his throat wanted to cry out.

"It isn't what I expected, Glory—what I dreamed of for years."

"But it's best—it seems best."

"I tried to make a place for you, too, but you wouldn't have it—you let it go; you preferred this other lot in life."

She remembered Josephs, and Sefton, and the newspaper, and the part, and she covered her face with her hands.

"How can I go on, Glory, to the peril of my—It's dangerous, even dangerous."

"Yes, you are a clergyman and I am an actress. You must think of that. People are so ignorant, so cruel, and I dare say they are talking already."

"Do you think I should care for that, Glory?" Her hands came down from her face. "Do you think I should care one jot if all the miserable scandal-mongering world thought——"

"You'll think the best of me, then?"

"I'll think of both of us as we used to be, my child, before the world came between us, before you——"

She was fighting against an impulse to fling herself into his arms, but she only said in a soft voice: "You are quite right, quite justified. I have chosen my lot in life, and must make the best of it."

"Well——" He was holding out his hand.

But nevertheless she put her hand behind her, thinking: "No; if I shake hands with him it will be the end of everything."

"Good-bye!" and with an expression of utter despair he left her.

She did not cry, and when Rosa came down immediately afterward she was smiling and her eyes were very bright.

"Was that your friend Mr. Storm? Yes? You must beware of him, my dear. He would stop your career and think he was doing God's service."

"There's no danger of that, Rosa. He only came to say he would come no more," and then something flashed in her eyes and died away, and then flashed again.

"Yes," thought Rosa, "there's an extraordinary attraction about her that makes all other women seem tame." And then Rosa remembered somebody else, and sighed.

John Storm went back to Soho by way of Clare Market, and when people saluted him in the streets with "Good-morning, Father," he did not answer because he did not see them. On going to church that night he came upon a group of Charlie's cronies betting six to one against his getting off, and a girl in gay clothes was waiting to speak to him. It was Aggie. She had come to plead for Charlie.

"It's the drink, sir. 'E's a good boy when 'e's not drinking. But I ask pardon for 'im; and if you would only not prosecute— —"

John was ashamed of himself at sight of the girl's fidelity to her unworthy lover.

"And you, my child—what about you?"

"Oh, I'm all right. What's broken can't be mended."

And meanwhile the church bells were ringing and the cabs were running to the theatres.

CHAPTER XIV

The rehearsals began early in the morning and usually lasted until late in the afternoon. Glory found them wearisome, depressing, and often humiliating. The body of the theatre was below the level of the street, and in the daytime was little better than a vast vault. If she entered by the front she stumbled against seats and saw the figures of men and women silhouetted in the distance, and heard the echo of cavernous voices. If by the back, she came upon the prompter's table set midway across the stage, with a twin gas-bracket shooting up behind it like a geyser, and an open space of some twenty feet by twenty in front whereon the imaginary passions were to disport themselves at play.

Glory found real ones among them, and they were sometimes in hideous earnest. Jealousy, envy, uncharitableness, and all the rancour of life where the struggle for it is bitterest, attempts to take advantage of her inexperience, to rob her of the best positions on the stage, to cut out her lines which "scored"—these, with the weary waits, the half darkness, the chill atmosphere, the void in front, with its seats in linen covers, suggesting an audience of silent ghosts, and then the sense of the bright, busy, bustling, rattling, real world above, sent her home day after day with a headache, a heartache, and tears bubbling out of her eyes.

And when she had conquered these conditions, or settled down to them, and had made such progress with her part as to throw away her scrip, the old horror of the woman she was to make herself into, came back as a new terror. The visionary Gloria was very proud and vain and selfish, and trampled everything under foot that she might possess the world and the things of the world.

Meantime the real Gloria had a far different part to play. Every morning, with a terrible reality at her heart, she glanced over the newspapers for news of John Storm. She had not far to look. A sort of grotesque romance had gathered about him, as of a modern Don Quixote tilting at windmills. His name was the point of a pun; there were cartoons, caricatures, and all other forms of the joke that is not a joke because it is an insult.

Sometimes she took stolen glances at his work. On Sunday morning she walked through Soho, past the people sitting on their doorsteps reading the sporting intelligence in the Sunday papers, with their larks in cages hung on nails, overhead, until she came to the church, and heard the singing inside, and saw chalked up on the walls the legend, "God bless the Farver!"

"Strange charge against a clergyman!" It was a low-class paper, and the charge was a badge of honour. A young ruffian (it was Charles Wilkes) had been brought up on remand on a charge of assaulting Father Storm, and being sentenced to a week's imprisonment, notwithstanding the Father's appeal and offer of bail, he had accused the clergyman of relations with his sweetheart (it was Agatha Jones).

Glory's anger at the world's treatment of John Storm deepened to a great love of the misunderstood and downtrodden man. She saw an announcement of his last service, and determined to go to it. The church was crowded, chiefly by the poor, and the air was heavy with the smell of oranges and beer. It was a week-day evening, and when the choir came in, followed by John Storm in his black cassock, Glory could not help a thrill of physical joy at being near him.

The text was, "Woe unto you, Scribes and Pharisees, hypocrites! for ye are like unto whited sepulchres, which indeed appear beautiful outside, but are within full of dead men's bones and all uncleanness!" The first half of the, sermon was a denunciation of the morality of men. We made clean the outside of the platter, but the so-called purity of England was a smug sham built upon rottenness and sin! There were men among us, damned sensualists, left untouched by the idleness of the public conscience, who did not even know where their children were to be found. Let them go down into the gutters of life and look for their own faces, and—God forgive them!—their mothers' faces, among the outcast and the criminal. The second half was a defence of woman. The sins of the world against women were the most crying wrongs of the time. Had they ever reflected on the heroism of women, on their self-denying, unrewarded labour? Oh, why was woman held so cheap as in this immoral London of to-day? There had been scarcely a breach of the law of Nature by women, and not one that men were not chiefly to blame for. Men tempted them by love of dress, of ease, of money, and of fame, to forget their proper vocation; but every true woman came right in the end, and preferred to the false and fictitious labour for worldly glory, a mother's silent and unseen devotion, counting it no virtue at all. "Yes, women, mothers, girls, in your hands lies the salvation of England. May you live in this prospect, and may God and his ever-blessed Mother be your reward all through this weary life and in glory everlasting!"

There was a procession with banners, cross, stars, green and blue fleur-de-lis, but Glory saw none of it. She was kneeling with her head down and heart choked with emotion. The next she knew the service was over, the congregation was gone; only one old woman in widow's weeds was left, jingling a bunch of keys.

"Has the Father gone?"

"No, ma'am; he is still in the sacristy."

"Show me to it."

At the next moment, with fluttering throat and a look of mingled love and awe, she was standing eye to eye with John Storm in the little bare chamber off the church.

"Glory, why do you come here?"

"I can't help it."

"But we said good-bye and parted."

"You did. I didn't. It was not so easy — —"

"Easy? I told you it wouldn't be easy, my child, and it hasn't been. I said I should suffer, and I have suffered. But I've borne it—you see I've borne it. Don't ask me at what cost."

"Oh, oh, oh!" and she covered her face.

"Yes, the devil tortured me with love first. I was seeing you and hearing you everywhere and in everything, Glory. But I got over that, and then he tortured me with remorse. I had left you to the mercy of the world. It was my duty to watch over you. I did it, too."

She glanced up quickly.

"Ah, you never knew that, but no matter! It's all over now, and I'm a different man entirely. But why do you come and torment me again? It's nothing to you, nothing at all. You can shake it off in a moment. That's your nature, Glory; you can't help it. But have you no pity? You find me here, trying to help the helpless—the brave girls who have the virtue to be poor, and the strength to be weak, and the courage to be friendless. Why can't you leave me alone? What am I to you? Nothing at all! You care nothing for me—nothing whatever."

She glanced up again, and the look of love in her eyes was stronger now than the look of awe. He saw it and could not help knowing how strongly it worked upon his feelings.

"Go back to your own world, unhappy girl! You love it—you must; you have sacrificed the best impulses of your heart to it!"

She was smiling now. It was the old radiant smile, but with a gleam of triumph in it that he had never seen before. It worked like madness upon him, and he tried to insult her again.

"Go back to your own company, to the people who *play* at real life, and build toy houses, and give themselves away body and soul for the clapping of hands in a theatre! Go back to the lies and hypocrisies of society, and the brainless, mashers who adorn it! They dance superbly, and are at home in drawing-rooms, and know all about sporting matters and theatrical affairs! I know none of these things, and I am kicked and cuffed and ridiculed and hounded down as an indecent man or shunned as a moral leper I Why do you come to me?" he cried, hoarse and husky.

But she only stretched out her hands to him and said, "Because I love you!"

"What are you saying?" He was quivering with pain.

"I love you, and have always loved you, and you love me—you know you do—you love me still!"

"Glory!"

"John!"

"For God's sake! Glory!"

With a wild shout of joy he rushed upon her, flung his arms about her, and covered her face and hands with kisses. After a moment he whispered, "Not here, not here!" and she felt too that the room was suffocating them, and they must go out into the open air, the fields, the park.

Somebody was knocking at the door. It was Mrs. Pincher. A man was waiting to speak to the Father. They found him in the lane. It was Jupe, the waiter. His simple face wore a strange expression of joy and fear, as if he wished to smile and dare not.

"My pore missis 'as got off and wants to come 'ome, sir, and I thought as you'd tell me what I oughter do."

"Take her back and forgive her, my man, that's the Christian course."

His love was now boundless; his large charity embraced everything, and going off he saluted everybody. "Good-evening, Mrs. Pincher.—Good-night, Lydia."

"Well, 'e *is* a Father, too, and no mistake!" somebody was saying behind him as he went away with Glory.

The moon was at the full, and while they were passing through the streets it struggled with the gas from the shop windows as the flame of a fire struggles with the sunshine, but when they passed under the trees it shone out in its white splendour like a bride. The immeasurable vault above was silvered with stars, too, through depth on depth of space, and all the glorious earth and heaven seemed to smile the smile of love. A strong south breeze was blowing, and as it shook the trees of the park, that blessed patch of Nature in the midst-of the toiling city seemed to sing the song of love!

Their hands found each other and they walked along almost in silence, afraid to break the spell of their dream lest they should awake and find it gone. It seemed wonderful to him that they were together, and he could hardly believe it was reality, though the touch of her hand filled him with a strange physical exultation which he had never felt before. He seemed to be walking on the clouds, and she too was swaying by his side as if her blood was dancing. Sometimes she dried her glistening eyes, and once she stopped and swung in front of him and looked long at him and then raised her face to his and kissed him.

"Whether you like it or not your life is bound up with mine for ever and ever!" she whispered.

"It had to be," he answered. "I know it now. I can no longer deceive myself."

"And we shall be happy? In spite of all you said we shall be very happy, eh?"

"Yes, that will be quite forgotten, Glory."

"And forgiven," she said, and then between a sigh and a blush she asked him to kiss her again.

"My love!"

"My soul!"

The wind swept the hood of her cape about her head and he could smell the fragrance of her hair.

He tried to think what he had done to deserve such happiness, but all the suffering he had gone through seemed as nothing compared to a joy like this. The great clock of Westminster swung its hollow sounds into the air, which went riding by on the wind like the notes of an organ, now full and now as soft as a baby's whisper. They could hear the far-off rumble of the vast city which fringed their blessed island like a mighty sea, and through the pulse of their clasped hands it seemed as if they felt the pulse of the world. An angel had come down and breathed on the face of the waters, and it was God's world, after all.

He took her home, and they parted at the door. "Don't come in to-night," she whispered. She wished to be alone, that she might think it all out and go over it again, every word, every look. There was a lingering hand-clasp and then she was gone.

He returned through the park and tried to step over the very places where her feet had trod. On reaching Buckingham Gate he turned back and walked round the park, and again round it, and yet again. The bells tolled out the hours, the cabs went westward with ladies in evening wraps going home from theatres, the tide of traffic ebbed farther and farther and died down, but still he walked and the wind sang to him.

"God can not blame us," he thought. "We were made to love each other." He uncovered his head to let the wind comb through his hair, and he was happy, happy, happy! Sometimes he shut his eyes, and then it was hard to believe that she was not walking by his side, a fragrant presence in the moonlight, going step by step with him.

When the day was near the wind had gone, the little world of wood was silent, and his footsteps crunched on the gravel. Then a yellow gleam came in the sky to the east, and a chill gust swept up as a scout before the dawn, the trees began to shiver, the surface of the lake to creep, the birds to call, and the world to stretch itself and yawn.

Peace in her chamber, wheresoe'er

It be—a holy place.

As he went home by Birdcage Walk the park was still heavy with sleep, and its homeless wanderers had not yet risen from their couches on the seats. A pale mist was lying over London, but the towers of the Abbey stood clear above it, and pigeons were wheeling around them like sea-fowl about rocks in the sea. What a night it had been! A night of dreams, of love, of rapture!

The streets were empty and very quiet—only the slow rattle of the dust-cart and the measured step of policemen changing beats. Long blue vistas and a cemetery silence as of a world under the great hand of the gentle brother of Death, and then the clang of Big Ben striking six.

A letter was waiting for John in the breathless hall. It was from the Bishop of London: "Come and see me at St. James's Square."

CHAPTER XV

Suddenly there sprang out to Glory the charm and fascination of the life she was putting away. Trying to be true to her altered relations with John Storm, she did not go to rehearsal the next morning—, but not yet having the courage of her new position, she did not tell Rosa her true reason for staying away. The part was exhausting—it tried her very much; a little break would do no harm. Rosa wrote to apologize for her on the score of health, and thus the first cloud of dissimulation rose up between them.

Two days passed, and then a letter came from the manager: "Trust you are rested and will soon be back. The prompter read your lines, but everything has gone to pieces. Slack, slovenly, spiritless, stupid, nobody acting, and nobody awake, it seems to me. 'All right at night, governor,' and the usual nonsense. Shows how much we want you. But envious people are whispering that you are afraid of the part. The blockheads! If you succeed this time you'll be made for life, my dear. And you *will* succeed! Yours merrily," etc.

With this were three letters addressed to the theatre. One of them was from a press-cutting agency asking to be allowed to supply all newspaper articles relating to herself, and inclosing a paragraph as a specimen: "A little bird whispers that 'Gloria,' as 'Gloria,' is to be a startling surprise. Those who have seen her rehearse——But mum's the word—an' we could an' we would," etc. Another of the letters was from the art editor of an illustrated weekly asking for a sitting to their photographer for a full-page picture; and the third inclosed the card of an interviewer on an evening paper. Only three days ago Glory would have counted all this as nothing, yet now she could not help but feel a thrilling, joyous excitement.

Drake called after the absence of a fortnight. He had come to speak of his last visit. His face was pale and serious, not fresh and radiant as usual, his voice was shaking and his manner nervous. Glory had never seen him exhibit so much emotion, and Rosa looked on in dumb astonishment.

"I was to blame," he said, "and I have come to say so. It was a cowardly thing to turn the man out of his church, and it was worse than cowardly to use you in doing it. Everything is fair, they say, in——" But he flushed up like a girl and stopped, and then faltered: "Anyhow, I'm sorry—very sorry; and if there is anything I can do——"

Glory tried to answer him, but her heart was beating violently, and she could not speak.

"In fact, I've tried to make amends already. Lord Robert has a living vacant in Westminster, and I've asked him to hand it over to the Bishop, with the request that Father Storm——"

"But will he?"

"I've told him he must. It's the least we can do if we are to have any respect for ourselves. And anyhow, I'm about tired of this anti-Storm uproar. It may be all very well far men like me to object to the man—I deny his authorities, and think him a man out of his century and country—but for these people with initials, who write in the religious papers, to rail at him, these shepherds who live on five thousand a year and pretend to follow One who hadn't a home or a second coat, and whose friends were harlots and sinners, though he was no sinner himself—it's infamous, it's atrocious, it raises my gorge against their dead creeds and paralytic churches. Whatever his faults, he is built on a large plan, he has the Christ idea, and he is a man and a gentleman, and I'm ashamed that I took advantage of him. That's all over now, and there's no help for it; but if I might hope that you will forgive—and forget——"

"Yes," said Glory in a low voice, and then there was silence, and when she lifted her head Drake was gone and Rosa was wiping her eyes.

"It was all for love of you, Glory. A woman can't hate a man when he does wrong for love of herself."

John Storm came in later the same day, when Rosa had gone out and Glory was alone. He was a different man entirely. His face looked round and his dark eyes sparkled. The clouds of his soul seemed to have drifted away, and he was boiling over with enthusiasm. He laughed constantly, and there was something almost depressing in the lumbering attempts at humour of the serious man.

"What do you think has happened? The Bishop sent for me and offered me a living in Westminster. It turns out to being the gift of Lord Robert Ure; but no thanks to him for it. Lady Robert was at the bottom of everything. She had called on the Bishop. He remembered me at the Brotherhood, and told me all about it. St. Jude's, Brown's Square, on the edge of the worst quarter in Christendom! It seems the Archdeacon expected it for Golightly, his son-in-law. The Reverend Joshua called on me this morning and tried to bully me, but I soon bundled him off to Botany Bay. Said the living had been promised to him—a lie, of course. I soon found that out. A lie is well named, you know—it hasn't a leg—to stand upon. Ha, ha, ha!"

Nothing would serve but that they should go to look at the scene of their future life, and with Don—he had brought his dog; it had to be held back from the pug under the table—they set off immediately. It was Saturday night, and as they dipped down into the slums that lie under the shadow of the Abbey, Old Pye Street, Peter's Street, and Duck Lane were aflare with the coarse lights of open naphtha lamps, and all but impassable with costers' barrows. There were the husky voices of the street hawkers, the hoarse laughter, the quarrelling, the oaths, the rasping shouts of the butcher selling chunks of dark joints by auction, the screeches of the roast-potato man, and the smell of stale vegetables and fried fish. "Jow, 'ow much a pound for yer turmaters?" "Three pence; I gave mor'n that for 'em myself." "Garn!" "S'elp me, Gawd, I did, mum!"

"Isn't it a glorious scene?" said John; and Glory, who felt chilled and sickened, recalled herself from some dream of different things altogether and said, "Isn't it?"

"Sanctuary, too! What human cats we are! The poor sinners cling to the place still!"

He took her into the alleys and courts that score and wrinkle the map of Westminster like an old man's face, and showed her the "model" lodging-houses and the gaudily decorated hells where young girls and soldiers danced and drank.

"What's the use of saying to these people, 'Don't drink; don't steal'? They'll answer, 'If you lived in these slums you would drink too.' But we'll show them that we can live here and do neither—that will be the true preaching."

And then he pictured a life of absolute self-sacrifice, which she was to share with him. "You'll manage all money matters, Glory. You can't think how I'm swindled. And then I'm such a donkey as far as money goes—that's not far with me, you know. Ha, ha, ha! Who's to find it? Ah, God pays his own debts. He'll see to that."

They were to live under the church itself; to give bread to the hungry and clothes to the naked; to set up their Settlement in the gaming-house of the Sharkeys, now deserted and shut up; to take in the *undeserving* poor—the people who had nothing to say for themselves, precisely those; and thus they were to show that they belonged neither to the publicans and sinners nor to the Scribes and Pharisees.

"Only let us get rid of self. Only let us show that self-interest never enters our head in one single thing we do——" and meantime Glory, who had turned her head aside with a lump in her throat, heard some one behind them saying:

"Lawd, Jow, that's the curick and his dorg—'im as got pore Sharkey took! See—'im with the laidy?"

"S'elp me, so it is! Another good man gorn to 'is gruel, and all 'long of a bloomin' dorg."

They walked round by the church. John was talking—rapturously at every step, and Glory was dragging after him like a criminal going to the pillory. At last they came out by Great Smith Street, and he cried: "See, there's the house of God under its spider's web of scaffolding, and here's the Broad Sanctuary—broad enough in all conscience! Look!"

A crowd of girls and men were trooping out of a place of entertainment opposite, and there were screams and curses. "Look at 'im!" cried a woman's voice. "There 'e is, the swine! And 'e was the ruin of me; and now 'e's 'listed for a soldier and going off with another woman!"

"You're bleedin' drunk, that's what you are!" said a man's voice, "and if you down't take kear I'll send ye 'ome on a dawer!"

"Strike me, will ye, ye dog? Do it! I dare you!"

"She ain't worth it, soldier—come along," said another female voice, whereupon the first broke into a hurricane of oaths; and a little clergyman going by at the moment—it was the Rev. J. Golightly—said: "Dear, dear! Are there no policemen about?" and so passed on, with his tall wife tucked under his arm.

John Storm pressed through the crowd and came between the two who were quarrelling. By the light of the lamp he could see them. The man was Charlie Wilkes, in the uniform of a soldier; the woman, with the paint running on her face, her fringe disordered, and her back hair torn down, was Aggie Jones.

"We down't want no religion 'ere," said Charlie, sneering.

"You'll get some, though, if you're not off quick!" said John. The man looked round for the dog and a moment afterward he had disappeared.

Glory came up behind. "O Aggie, woman, is it you?" she said, and then the girl began to cry in a drunken sob.

"Girls is cruel put upon, mum," said one of the women; and another cried, "Nix, the slops!" and a policeman came pushing his way and saying: "Now, then, move on! We ain't going to stand 'ere all night."

"Call a cab, officer," said John.

"Yes sir—certainly, Father. Four-wheel-er!"

"Where do you live, Aggie?" said Glory; but the girl, now sobbing drunk, was too far gone to follow her.

"She lives in Brown's Square, sir," said the woman who had spoken before, and when the cab came up she was asked to get in with the other three.

It was a tenement house, fronting to one facade of St. Jude's, and Aggie's room was on the second story. She was helpless, and John carried her up the stairs. The place was in hideous disorder, with clothing lying about on chairs, underclothing scattered on the floor, the fire out, many cigarette ends in the fender, a candle stuck in a beer bottle, and a bunch of withered roses on the table.

As John laid the girl on the bed she muttered, "Lemme alone!" and when he asked what was to happen to her when she grew old if she behaved like this when young, she mumbled: "Don't want to be old. Who's goin' to like me then, d'ye think?"

Half an hour afterward Glory and John were passing through the gates into Clement's Inn, with its moonlight and silence, its odour of moistened grass, its glimpse of the stars, and the red and white blinds of its windows lit up round about. John was still talking rapturously. He was now picturing the part which Glory was to play in the life they were to live together. She was to help and protect their younger sisters, the child-women, the girls in peril, to enlist their loyalty and filial tenderness for the hour of temptation.

"Won't it be glorious? To live the life, the real life of warfare with the world's wickedness and woe! Won't it be magnificent? You'll do it too! You'll go down into those slums and sloughs which I've shown you to-night—they are the cradle of shame and sin, Glory, and this wicked London rocks it!—you'll go down into them like a ministering angel to raise the fallen and heal the wounded! You'll live in them, revel in them, rejoice in them, they'll be your battlefield. Isn't that better, far better, a thousand times better, than *playing* at life, and all its fashions and follies and frivolities?"

Glory struggled to acquiesce, and from time to time in a trembling voice she said "Yes," and "Oh, yes," until they came to the door of the Garden House, and then a strange thing happened. Somebody was singing in the drawing-room to the music of the piano. It was Drake. The window was open and his voice floated over the moonlit gardens;

Du liebes Kind, komm' geh mit mir!

Gar schöne Spiele spiel' ich mit dir.

Suddenly it seemed to Glory that two women sprang into life in her—one who loved John Storm and wished to live and work beside him, the other who loved the world and felt that she could never give it up. And these two women were fighting for her heart, which should have it and hold it and possess it forever.

She looked up at John, and he was smiling triumphantly, "Are you happy?" she asked.

"Happy! I know a hundred men who are a hundred times as rich as I, but not one who is a hundredth part as happy!"

"Darling!" she whispered, holding back her tears. Then looking away from him she said, "And do you really think I'm good enough for a life of such devotion and self-sacrifice?"

"Good enough!" he cried, and for a moment his merry laughter drowned the singing overhead.

"But will the world think so?"

"Assuredly. But who cares what the world thinks?"

"We do, dear—we must!"

And then, while the song went on, she began to depreciate herself in a low voice and with a creeping sense of hypocrisy—to talk of her former life in London as a danger, of the tobacco-shop, the foreign clubs, the music hall, and all the mire and slime with which she had been besmirched. "Everything is known now, dear. Have you never thought of this? It is your duty to think of it."

But he only laughed again with a joyous voice. "What's the odds?" he said. "The world is made up for the most part of low, selfish, sensual beings, incapable of belief in noble aims. Every innovator in such a world exposes himself to the risk of being slandered or ridiculed, or even shut up in a lunatic asylum. But who wouldn't rather be St. Theresa in her cell than Catharine of Russia on her throne? And in your case, what does it come to anyway? Only that you've gone through the fiery furnace and come out unscathed. All the better—you'll be a living witness, a proof that it is possible to pass through this wicked Babylon unharmed and untouched."

"Yes, if I were a man—but with a woman it is so different! It is an honour to a man to have conquered the world, but a disgrace to a woman to have fought with it. Yes, believe me, I know what I'm saying. That's the cruel tragedy in a woman's life, do what you will to hide it. And then you are so much in the eye of the world; and besides your own position there is your family's, your uncle's. Think what it would be if the world pointed the finger of scorn at your—at your mission—at your high and noble aims—and all on account of me! You would cease to love me-and I—I——"

"Listen!" He had been shuffling restlessly on the pavement before her. "Here I stand! Here are you! Let the waves of public opinion dash themselves against us—we stand or fall together!" "Oh, oh, oh!"

She was crying on his breast, but with what mixed and conflicting feelings! Joy, pain, delight, dread, hope, disappointment. She had tried to dishonour herself in his eyes, and it would have broken her heart if she had succeeded. But she had failed and he had triumphed, and that was harder still to bear.

From overhead they heard the last lines of the song:

> *Erreicht den Hof mit Müh und Noth*
>
> *In seinen Armen das Kind war todt.*

"Good-night," she whispered, and fled into the house. The lights in the dining-room were lowered, but she found a telegram that was waiting on the mantelpiece. It was from Sefton, the manager: "Author arrived in London today. Hopes to be at rehearsal Monday. Please be there certain."

The world was seizing her again, the imaginary Gloria was dragging her back with visions of splendour and success. But she crept upstairs and went by the drawing-room on tip-toe. "Not to-night," she thought. "My face is not fit to be seen to-night."

There was a dying fire in her bedroom, and her evening gown had been laid out on a chair in front of it. She put the gown away in a drawer, and out of a box which she drew from beneath the bed she took a far different costume. It was the nurse's outdoor cloak, which she had bought for use at the hospital. She held it a moment by the tips of her fingers and looked at it, and then put it back with a sigh.

"Gloria! is that you?" Rosa called up the stairs; and Drake's cheery voice cried, "Won't our nightingale come down and give us a stave before I go?"

"Too late! Just going to bed. Good-night," she answered. Then she lit a candle and sat down to write a letter.

"It's no use, dear John, I can not! It would be like putting bad money into the offertory to put me into that holy work. Not that I don't admire it, and love it, and worship it. It is the greatest work in the world, and last week I thought I could count everything else as dross, only remembering that I loved you and that nothing else mattered. But now I know that this was a vain and fleeting sentiment, and that the sights and scenes of your work repel me on a nearer view, just as the hospital repelled me in the early mornings when the wards were being cleaned and the wounds dressed, and before the flowers were laid about.

"Oh, forgive me, forgive me! But if I am fit to join your life at all it can not be in London. That 'old serpent called the devil and Satan' would be certain to torment me here. I could not live within sight and sound of London and go on with the life you live. London would drag me back. I feel as if it were an earlier lover, and I must fly away from it. Is that possible? Can we go elsewhere? It is a monstrous demand, I know. Say you can not agree to it. Say so at once—it will serve me right."

The stout watchman of the New Inn was calling midnight when Glory stole out to post her letter. It fell into the letter-box with a thud, and she crept back like a guilty thing.

CHAPTER XVI

Next morning Mrs. Callender heard John Storm singing to himself before he left his bedroom, and she was standing at the bottom of the stairs when he came down three steps at a time.

"Bless me, laddie," she said, "to see your face shining a body would say that somebody had left ye a legacy or bought ye a benefice instead of taking your church frae ye!"

"Why, yes, and better than both, and that's just what I was going to tell you."

"You must be in a hurry to do it, too, coming downstairs like a cataract."

"You came down like a cataract yourself once on a time, auntie; I'll lay my life on that."

"Aye, did I, and not sae lang since neither. And fools and prudes cried 'Oh!' and called me a tomboy. But, hoots; I was nought but a body born a wee before her time. All the lasses are tomboys now, bless them, the bright heart-some things!"

"Auntie," said John softly, seating himself at the breakfast table, "what d'ye think?"

She eyed him knowingly. "Nay, I'm ower thrang working to be bothered thinking. Out with it, laddie."

He looked wise. "Don't you remember saying—that work like mine wanted a woman's hand in it?"

Her old eyes blinked. "Maybe I did, but what of it?"

"Well, I've taken your advice, and now a woman's hand is coming into it to guide it and direct it."

"It must be the right hand, though, mind that."

"It *will* be the right hand, auntie."

"Weel, that's grand," with another twinkle. "I thought it might be the *left*, ye see, and ye might be putting a wedding-ring on it!" And then she burst into a peal of laughter.

"However did you find it out?" he said, with looks of astonishment.

"Tut, laddie, love and a cough can not be hidden. And to think a woman couldna see through you, too! But come," tapping the table with both hands, "who is she?"

"Guess."

"Not one of your Sisters—no?" with hesitation.

"No," with emphasis.

"Some other simpering thing, na doot-they're all alike these days."

"But didn't you say the girls were all tomboys now?"

"And if I did, d'ye want a body to be singing the same song always? But come, what like is she? When I hear of a lassie I like fine to know her colour first. What's her complexion?"

"Guess again."

"Is she fair? But what a daft auld dunce I am!—to be sure she's fair."

"Why, how did you know that, now?"

"Pooh! They say a dark man is a jewel in a fair woman's eye, and I'll warrant it's as true the other way about. But what's her name?"

John's face suddenly straightened and he pretended not to hear.

"What's her name?" stamping with both feet.

"Dear me, auntie, what an ugly old cap you're wearing!"

"Ugly?" reaching up to the glass. "Who says it's ugly?"

"I do."

"Tut! you're only a bit boy, born yesterday. But, man, what's all this botherment about telling a lassie's name?"

"I'll bring her to see you, auntie."

"I should think you will, indeed! and michty quick, too!"

This was on Sunday, and by the first post on Monday John Storm received Glory's letter. It fell on him like a blast out of a cloud in the black northeast, and cut him to the heart's core. He read it again, and being alone he burst into laughter. He took it up a third time, and when he had finished there was something at his throat that seemed to choke him. His first impulse was fury. He wanted to rush off to Glory and insult her, to ask her if she was mad or believed him to be so. Because she was a coward herself, being slave-bound to the world and afraid to fight it face to face, did she wish to make a coward of him also—to see him sneak away from the London that had kicked him, like a cur with its tail between its legs?

After this there came an icy chill and an awful consciousness that mightier forces were at work than any mere human weakness. It was the world itself, the great pitiless world, that was dividing them again as it had divided them before, but irrevocably now-not as a playful nurse that puts petted children apart, but as a torrent that tears the cliffs asunder. "Leave the world, my son, and return to your unfinished vows." Could it be true that this was only another reminder of his broken obedience?

Then came pity. If Glory was slave-bound to the world, which of us was not in chains to something? And the worst slavery of all was slavery to self. But that was an abyss he dared not look into; and he began to think tenderly of Glory, to tell himself how much she had to sacrifice, to remember his anger and to be ashamed.

A week passed, and he went about his work in a helpless way, like a derelict without rudder or sail and with the sea roaring about it. Every afternoon when he came home from Soho Mrs. Callender would trip into the hall wearing a new cap with a smart bow, and finding that he was alone she would say, "Not to-day, then?"

"Not to-day," he would answer, and they would try to smile. But seeing the stamp of suffering on his face, she said at last, "Tut, laddie! they love too much who die for love."

On the Sunday afternoon following he turned again toward Clement's Inn. He had come to a decision at last, and was calm and even content, yet his happiness was like a gourd which had grown up in a day, and the morrow's sun had withered it.

Glory had been to rehearsal every day that week. Going to the theatre on Monday night she had said to herself, "There can be no harm in rehearsing—I'm not compelled to play." Notwithstanding her nervousness, the author had complimented her on her passion and self-abandonment, and going home she had thought: "I might even go through the first performance and then give it all up. If I had a success, that would be beautiful, splendid, almost heroic—it would be thrilling to abandon everything." Not hearing from John, she told herself he must be angry, and she felt sorry for him. "He doesn't know yet how much I am going to do." Thus the other woman in her tempted and overcame her, and drew her on from day to day.

Mrs. Macrae sent Lord Robert to invite her to luncheon on Sunday. "There can be no harm in going there," she thought. She went with Rosa, and was charmed with the lively, gay, and brilliant company. Clever and beautiful women, clever and handsome men, and nearly all of them of her own profession. The mistress of the mansion kept open house after church parade on Sunday, and she sat at the bottom of her table, dressed in black velvet, with the Archdeacon on her right and a famous actor on her left. Lord Robert sat at the head and talked to a lady whose remarks were heard all over the room; but Lady Robert was nowhere to be seen; there was a hush when her name was mentioned, and then a whispered rumour that she had differences with her husband, and had scandalized her mother by some act of indiscretion.

Glory's face beamed, and for the first half-hour she seemed to be on the point of breaking into a rapturous "Well!" Nearly opposite to her at the table sat a lady whose sleepy look and drowsy voice and airs of languor showed that she was admired, and that she knew it. Glory found her very amusing, and broke into little trills of laughter at her weary, withering comments. This drew the attention of some of the men; they found the contrast interesting. The conversation consisted first of hints, half signs, brilliant bits of by-play, and Glory rose to it like a fish to the May-fly. Then it fell upon bicycling and the costumes ladies wore for it. The languid one commented upon the female fetich, the skirt, and condemned "bloomers," whereupon Glory declared that they were just charming, and being challenged (by a gentleman) for her reasons she said, "Because when a girl's got them on she feels as if she's an understudy for a man, and may even have a chance of playing the part itself in another and a better world."

Then there was general laughter, and the gentleman said, "You're in the profession yourself now, aren't you?"

"Just a stranger within your gates," she answered; and when the talk turned on a recent lawsuit, and the languid one said it was inconceivable that the woman concerned could have been such a coward in relation to the man, Glory protested that it was just as natural for a woman to be in fear of a man (if she loved him) as to be afraid of a mouse or to look under the bed.

"*Ma chère*," said a dainty little lady sitting next but one (she had come to London to perform in a silent play), "they tells me you's half my countrywoman. All right. Will you not speak de French to poor me?" And when Glory did so the little one clapped her hands and declared she had never heard the English speak French before.

"Say French-cum-Irish," said Glory, "or, rather, French which begat Irish, which begat Manx!"

"Original, isn't she?" said somebody who was laughing.

"Like a sea-gull among so many pigeons!" said somebody else, and the hothouse airs of the languid lady were lost as in a fresh gust from the salt sea.

But her spirits subsided the moment she had recrossed the threshold. As they were going home in the cab, past the hospital and down Piccadilly. Rosa, who was proud and happy, said: "There! All society isn't stupid and insipid, you see; and there are members of your own profession who try to live up to the ideal of moral character attainable by a gentleman in England even yet."

"Yes, no doubt... But, Rosa, there's another kind of man altogether, whose love has the reverence of a religion, and if I ever meet a man like that—one who is ready to trample all the world under his feet for me—I think—yes, I really think I shall leave everything behind and follow him."

"Leave everything behind, indeed! That *would* be pretty! When everything yields before you, too, and all the world and his wife are waiting to shout your praises!"

Rosa had gone to her office, and Glory was turning over some designs for stage costumes, when Liza came in to say that the "Farver" was coming upstairs.

"He has come to scold me," thought Glory, so she began to hum, to push things about, and fill the room with noise. But when she saw his drawn face and wide-open eyes she wanted to fall on his neck and cry.

"You have come to tell me you can't do what I suggested?" she said. "Of course you can't."

"No," he said slowly, very slowly. "I have thought it all over, and concluded that I can—that I must. Yes, I am willing to go away, Glory, and when you are ready I shall be ready too."

"But where—where—?"

"I don't know yet; but I am willing to wait for the unrolling of the scroll. I am willing to follow step by step, not knowing whither. I am willing to go where God wills, for life or death."

"But your work in London—your great, great work——"

"God will see to that, Glory. He can do without any of us. None of us can do without him. The sun will set without any assistance, you know," and the pale face made an effort to smile.

"But, John, my dear, dear John, this is not what you expected, what you have been thinking of and dreaming of, and building your hopes upon."

"No," he said; "and for your sake I am sorry, very sorry. I thought of a great career for you, Glory. Not rescue work merely—others can do that. There are many good women in the world—nearly all women are good, but Jew are great—and for the salvation of England, what England wants now is a great woman.... As for me—God knows best! He has his own way of weaning us from vanity and the snares of the devil. You were only an instrument in his hands, my child, hardly knowing what you were doing. Perhaps he has a work of intercession for us somewhere—far away from here—in some foreign mission field—who can say?"

A feeling akin to terror caught her breath, and she looked up at him with tearful eyes.

"After all, I am glad that this has happened," he said. "It will help me to conquer self, to put self behind my back forever, to show the world, by leaving London, that self has not entered into my count at all, and that I am thinking of nothing but my work."

A warm flush rose to her cheeks as he spoke, and again she wanted to fling herself on his neck and cry. But he was too calm for that, too sad and too spiritual. When he rose to go she held out her hands to him, but he only took them and carried them to his lips, and kissed them.

As soon as she was alone she flung herself down and cried, "Oh, give me strength to follow this man, who mistakes his love of me for the love of God!" But even while she sat with bent head and her hands over her face the creeping sense came back as of another woman within her who was fighting for her heart. She had conquered again, but at what a cost! The foreign mission field—what associations had she with that? Only the memory of her father's lonely life and friendless death.

She was feeling cold and had begun to shiver, when the door opened and Rosa entered.

"So he *did* come again?"

"Yes."

"I thought he would," and Rosa laughed coldly.

"What do you mean?"

"That when religious feelings take possession of a man he will stop at nothing to gain the end he has in view."

"Rosa," said Glory, flushing crimson, "if you imply that my friend is capable of one unworthy act or thought I must ask you to withdraw your words absolutely and at once!"

"Very well, dear. I was only thinking for your own good. We working women must not ruin our lives or let anybody else ruin them. 'Duty,' 'self-sacrifice'—I know the old formulas, but I don't believe in them. Obey your own heart, my dear, that is your first duty. A man like Storm would take you out of your real self, and stop your career, and——"

"Oh, my career, my career! I'm tired to death of hearing of it!"

"Glory!"

"And who knows? I may not go on with it, after all."

"If you have lost your sense of duty to yourself, have you forgotten your duty to Mr. Drake? Think what Mr. Drake has done for you!"

"Mr. Drake! Mr. Drake! I'm sick of that too."

"How strange you are to-night, Glory!"

"Am I? So are you. It is Mr. Drake here and Mr. Drake there! Are you trying to force me into his arms?"

"Is it you that says that, Glory—you? and to me, too? Don't you see that this is a different case altogether? And if I thought of my own feelings only—consulted my own heart——"

"Rosa!"

"Ah! Is it so very foolish? Yes, he is young and handsome, and rich and brilliant, while I—I am ridiculous."

"No, no, Rosa; I don't mean that."

"I do, though; and when you came in between us—young and beautiful and clever—everything that I was not, and could never hope to be—and he was so drawn to you—what was I to do? Nurse my hopeless and ridiculous love—or think of him—his happiness?"

"Rosa, my poor dear Rosa, forgive me! forgive me!"

An hour later, dinner being over, they had returned to the drawing-room. Rosa was writing at the table, and there was no sound in the room except the scratching of her pen, the falling of the slips of "copy," and the dull reverberation of the bell of St. Clement's Danes, which was ringing for evening service. Glory was sitting at the desk by the window, with her head on her hands, looking down into the garden. Out of the dead load at her heart she kept saying to herself: "Could I do that? Could I give up the one I loved for his own good, putting myself back, and thinking of him only?" And then a subtle hypocrisy stole over her and she thought, "Yes I could, I could!" and in a fever of nervous excitement she began to write a letter:

"The wind bloweth where it listeth, and so with a woman's will. I can not go abroad with you, dear, because I can not allow myself to break up your life, for it *would* be that—it would, it would, you know it would! There are ten thousand men good enough for the foreign mission field, but there is only one man in the world for your work in London. This is one of the things hidden from the wise, and revealed to children and fools. It would be wrong of me to take you away from your great scene. I daren't do it. It would be too great a responsibility. My conscience must have been dead and buried when I suggested such a possibility! Thank God, it has had a resurrection, and it is not yet too late."

But when the letter was sealed and stamped, and sent out to the post, she thought: "I must be mad, and there is no method in my madness either. What do I want—to join his life in London?" And then remembering what she had written, it seemed as if the other woman must have written it—the visionary woman, the woman she was making herself into day by day.

CHAPTER XVII

John Storm had left home early on Monday morning. It was the last day of his tenancy of the clergy-house, and there was much to do at Soho. Toward noon he made his way to the church in Bishopsgate Street for the first time since he had left the Brotherhood. It was midday service, and the little place was full of business men with their quick, eyes and eager faces. The Superior preached, and the sermon was on the religious life. We were each composed of two beings, one temporal, the other eternal, one carnal, the other spiritual. Life was a constant warfare between these two nearly matched forces, and often the victory seemed to sway from this side to that. Our enemy with the chariots of iron was ourselves. There was a Judas in each one of us ready to betray us with a kiss if allowed. The lusts of the flesh were the most deadly sins, absolute chastity the most pleasing to God of all virtues. Did we desire to realize what the religious life could be? Then let us reflect upon the news which had come from the South Seas. What was the word that had fallen that morning on all Christendom like a thunderclap, say, rather, like the blast of a celestial trumpet? Father Damien was dead! Think of his lonely life in that distant island where doomed men lived out their days. Cut off from earthly marriage, with no one claiming his affection in the same way as Christ, he was free to commit himself entirely to God and to God's afflicted children. He was truly married to Christ. Christ occupied his soul as Lord and spouse. Glorious life! Glorious death! Eternal crown of glory waiting for him in the glory everlasting!

When the service ended John Storm stepped up to speak to the Father. His wide-open eyes were flaming; he was visibly excited. "I came to ask a question," he said, "but it is answered already. I will follow Father Damien and take up his work. I was thinking of the mission field, but my doubt was whether God had called me, and I had great fear of going uncalled. God brought me here this morning, not knowing what I was to do, but now I know, and my mind is made up at last."

The Father was not less moved. They went out into the courtyard together and walked to and fro, planning, scheming, contriving, deciding.

"You'll take the vows first, my son?"

"The vows?"

"The life vows."

"But—but will that be necessary?"

"It will be best. Think what a peculiar appeal it have for those poor doomed creatures! They are cut off from the world by a terrible affliction, but you will be cut off by the graciousness of a Christ-fed purity. They are lepers made of disease; you will be as a leper for the kingdom of heaven's sake."

"But, Father—if that be so—how much greater the appeal will be if—if a woman goes out also! Say she is young and beautiful and of great gifts?"

"Brother Andrew may go with you, my son."

"Yes, Brother Andrew as well. But holy men in all ages have been bound by ties of intimacy and affection to good women who have lived and worked beside them."

"Sisters, my son, elder sisters always."

"And why not? Sister, indeed, and united to me by a great and spiritual love."

"We are none of us invincible, my son; let us not despise danger."

"Danger, Father! What is the worth of my religion if it does not enable me to defy that?"

"Well, well—do not decide too soon. I'll come to you at Soho this evening."

"Do. It's our last night there. I must tell my poor people what my plans are to be. Good-bye for the present, Father, good-bye."

"Good-bye, my son," and as John Storm went off with a light heart and bounding step the Father passed indoors with downcast face, saying to himself with a sigh, "Let him that thinketh he standeth take heed lest he fall."

It was Lord Mayor's Day again, the streets were thronged, and John Storm was long in forging his way home. Glory's letter was waiting for him, and he tore it open with nervous fingers, but when he had read it he laughed aloud. "God bless her! But she doesn't know everything yet." Mrs. Callender was out in the carriage; she would be back for lunch, and the maid was laying the cloth; but he would not wait. After scribbling a few lines in pencil to tell of his great resolve, he set off to Clement's Inn. The Strand was less crowded when he returned to it, and the newsboys were calling the evening papers with "Full Memoir of Father Damien."

On coming home from rehearsal Glory had found the costume for her third act, her great act, awaiting her. All day long she had been thinking of her letter to John, half ashamed of it, half regretting it, almost wishing it could be withdrawn. But the dress made a great tug at her heart, and she could not resist the impulse to try it on. The moment she had done so the visionary woman whose part she was to play seemed to take possession of her, and shame and regret were gone.

It was a magnificent stage costume, green as the grass in spring with the morning sun on it. The gown was a splendid brocade with gold-embroidered lace around the square-cut neck and about the shoulders of the tight-made sleeves. Round her hips was a sash of golden tissue, and its hanging ends were fringed with emeralds. A band of azure stones encircled her head, and her fingers were covered with turquoise rings.

She went to the drawing-room, shut the door, and began to rehearse the scene. It was where the imaginary Gloria, being vain and selfish, trampled everything under her feet that she might possess the world and the things of the world. Glory spoke the words aloud, forgetting they were not her own, until she heard another voice saying, "May I come in, dear?"

It was John at the door. She was ashamed of her costume then, but there was no running away. "Yes, of course, come in," she cried, trembling all over, half afraid to be seen, and yet proud too of her beauty and her splendour. When he entered she was laughing nervously and was about to say, "See, this has happened before— —"

But he saw nothing unusual, and she was disappointed and annoyed. Coming in breathless, as if he had been running, he flung himself down on one end of the couch, threw his hat on the other end, and said: "What did I tell you, Glory? That a way would open itself, and it has!"

"Really?"

"Didn't you think of it when you saw the news in the papers this morning?"

"What news?"

"That Father Damien is dead."

"But can you—do you really mean that—do you intend— —"

"I do, Glory—I do."

"Then you didn't get my letter this morning?"

"Oh, yes, dear, yes; but you were only thinking for me—God bless you!—that I was giving up a great scene for a little one. But this—this is the greatest scene in the world, Glory. Life is a small sacrifice; the true sacrifice is a living death, a living crucifixion."

She felt as if he had taken her by the throat and was choking her. He had got up and was walking to and fro, talking impetuously.

"Yes, it is a great sacrifice I am asking you to make now, dear. That far-off island, the poor lepers, and then lifelong banishment. But God will reward you, and with interest too. Only think, Glory! Think of the effect of your mere presence out there among those poor doomed creatures! A young and beautiful woman! Not a melancholy old dolt like me, preaching and prating to them, but a bright and brilliant girl, laughing with them, playing games with them, making mimicry for them, and singing to them in the voice of an angel. Oh, they'll love you, Glory, they'll worship you—you'll be next to God and his blessed mother with them. And already I hear them saying among themselves: 'Heaven bless her! She might have had the world at her feet and made a great name and a great fortune, but she gave it all up—all, all, all—for pity and love of us!' Won't it be glorious, my child? Won't it be the noblest thing in all the world?"

And she struggled to answer, "Yes, no doubt—the noblest thing in all the world!"

"Then you agree? Ah, I knew your heart spoke in your first letter, and you wanted to leave London. You shall, too, for God has willed it."

Then she recovered a little and made a nervous attempt to withdraw. "But the church at Westminster?"

He laughed like a boy. "Oh, Golightly may have that now, and welcome."

"But the work in London?"

"Ah, that's all right, Glory. Ever since I heard from you I have been dealing with the bonds which bound me to London one by one, unravelling some and breaking others. They are all discharged now, every one of them, and I need think of them no more. Self is put behind forever, and I can stand before God and say: 'Do with me as you will; I am ready for anything—anything!'"

"Oh!"

"Crying, Glory? My poor, dear child! But why are you crying?"

"It's nothing!"

"Are you sure—quite sure? Am I asking too much of you? Don't let us deceive ourselves—think——"

"Let us talk of something else now." She began to laugh. "Look at me, John—don't I look well to-day?"

"You always look well, Glory."

"But isn't there any difference—this dress, for instance?"

Then his sight came back and his big eyes sparkled. "How beautiful you are, dear!"

"Really? Do I look nice then—really?"

"My beautiful, beautiful girl!"

Her head was thrown back, and she glowed with joy.

"Don't come too near me, you know—don't crush me."

"Nay, no fear of that—I should be afraid."

"Not that I mustn't be touched exactly."

"What will they think, I wonder, those poor, lost creatures, so ugly, so disfigured?"

"And my red hair. This colour suits it, doesn't it?"

"Some Madonna, they'll say; the very picture of the mother of God herself!"

"Are you—are you afraid of me in this frock, dear? Shall I run and take it off?"

"No—no; let me look at you again."

"But you don't like me to-day, for all that."

"I?"

"Do you know you've never once kissed me since you came into the room?"

"Glory!"

"My love! my love!"

"And you," he said, close to her lips, "are you ready for anything?"

"Anything," she whispered.

At the next moment she was holding herself off with her arms stiff about his neck, that she might look at him and at her lace sleeves at the same time. Suddenly a furrow crossed his brow. He had remembered the Father's warning, and was summoning all his strength.

"But out there I'll love you as a sister, Glory."

"Ah!"

"For the sake of those poor doomed beings cut off from earthly love we'll love each other as the angels love."

"Yes, that is the highest, purest, truest love, no doubt. Still——"

"What does the old Talmud say?—'He who divorces himself from the joys of earth weds himself to the glories of Paradise.'"

Her lashes were still wet; she was gazing deep into his eyes.

"And to think of being united in the next world, Glory—what happiness, what ecstasy!"

"Love me in this world, dearest," she whispered.

"You'll be their youth, Glory, their strength, their loveliness!"

"Be mine, darling, be mine!"

But the furrow crossed his brow a second time, and he disengaged himself before their lips had met again. Then he walked about the room as before, talking in broken sentences. They would have to leave soon—very soon—almost at once. And now he must go back to Soho. There was so much to do, to arrange. On reaching the door he hesitated, quivering with love, hardly knowing how to part from her. She was standing with head down, half angry and half ashamed.

"Well, *au revoir*," he cried in a strained voice, and then fled down the stairs. "The Father was right," he thought. "No man is invincible. But, thank God, it is over! It can never occur again!"

Her glow had left her, and she felt chilled and lost There was no help for it now, and escape was impossible. She must renounce everything for the man who had renounced everything for her. Sitting on the couch, she dropped her head on the cushion and cried like a child. In the lowest depths of her soul she knew full well that she could never go away, but she began to bid good-bye in her heart to the life she had been living. The charm and fascination of London began to pass before her like a panorama, with all the scenes of misery and squalor left out. What a beautiful world she was leaving behind her! She would remember it all her life long with useless and unending regret. Her tears were flowing through the fingers which were clasped beneath her face.

A postman's knock came to the door downstairs. The letter was from the manager, written in the swirl and rush of theatrical life, and reading like a telegram: "Theatre going on rapidly, men working day and night, rehearsals advanced and scenery progressing; might we not fix this day fortnight for the first performance?"

Inclosed with this was a letter from the author: "You are on the eve of an extraordinary success, dear Gloria, and I write to reassure and congratulate you. Some signs of inexperience I may perhaps observe, some lack of ease and simplicity, but already it is a performance of so much passion and power that I predict for it a triumphant success. A great future awaits you. Don't shrink from it, don't be afraid of it; it is as certain as that the sun will rise to-morrow."

She carried the letter to her lips, then rose from the couch, and threw up her head, closed her eyes, and smiled. The visionary woman was taking hold of her again with the slow grip and embrace of the glacier.

Rosa came home to dine, and at sight of the new costume she cried, "Shade of Titian, what a picture!" During dinner she mentioned that she had met Mr. Drake, who had said that the Prince was likely to be present at the production, having asked for the date and other particulars.

"But haven't you heard the *great* news, dear? It's in all the late editions of the evening papers."

"What is it?" said Glory; but she saw what was coming.

"Father Storm is to follow Father Damien. That's the report, at all events; but he is expected to make a statement at his club to-night, and I have to be there for the paper."

As soon as dinner was over Rosa went off to Soho, and then Glory was brought back with a shock to the agony of her inward struggle. She knew that her hour had arrived, and that on her action now everything depended. She knew that she could never break the chains by which the world and her profession held her. She knew that the other woman had come, that she must go with her, and go for good. But the renunciation of love was terrible. The day had been soft and beautiful. It was falling asleep and yawning now, with a drowsy breeze that shook the yellow leaves as they hung withered and closed on the thinning boughs like the fingers of an old maid's hand. She was sitting at the desk by the window, trying to write a letter. More than once she tore up the sheet, dried her eyes, and began again. What she wrote last was this:

"It is impossible, dear John. I can not go with you to the South Seas. I have struggled, but I can not, I can not! It is the greatest, noblest, sublimest mission in the world, but I am not the woman for these high tasks. I should be only a fruitless fig tree, a sham, a hypocrite. It would be like taking a dead body with you to take me, for my heart would not be there. You would find that out, dear, and I should be ashamed.

"And then I can not leave this life—I can not give up London. I am like a child—I like the bustling streets, the brilliant thoroughfares, the crowds, the bands of music, the lights at night, and the sense of life. I like to succeed, too, and to be admired, and—yes, to hear the clapping of hands in a theatre. You are above all this, and can look down at it as dross, and I like you for that also. But give it all up I can't; I haven't the strength; it is in my blood, dear, and if I part from it I must die.

"And then I like to be fondled and coaxed and kissed, and I want so much—oh, so much to be loved! I want somebody to tell me every day and always how much he loves me, and to praise me and pet me and forget everything else for me, everything, everything, even his own soul and salvation! You can not do that; it would be sinful, and besides it wouldn't be love as you understand it, and as it ought to be, if you are to go out to that solemn and awful task.

"When I said I loved you I spoke the truth, dear, and yet I didn't know what the word meant really, I didn't realize everything. I love you still—with all my heart and soul I love you; but now I know that there is a difference between us, that we can never come together. No, I can not reach up to your austere heights. I am so weak; you are so strong. Your 'strength is as the strength of ten because your heart is pure,' while I——

"I am unworthy of your thoughts, John. Leave me to the life I have chosen. It may be poor and vain and worthless, but it is the only life I'm fit for. And yet I love you—and you loved me. I suppose God makes men and women like that sometimes, and it is no use struggling.

"One kiss, dear—it is the last."

CHAPTER XVIII

John Storm went back to Victoria Square with a bright and joyful face and found Mrs. Callender waiting for him, grim as a judge. He could see that her eyes were large and red with weeping, but she fell on him instantly with withering scorn.

"So you're here at last, are ye? A pretty senseless thing this is, to be sure! What are you dreaming about? Are you bewitched or what? Do you suppose things can be broken off in this way? You to go to the leper islands indeed!"

"I'm called, auntie, and when God calls a man, what can he do but answer with Samuel——"

"Tut! Don't talk sic nonsense. Besides, Samuel had some sense. He waited to be called three times, and I havena heard this is your third time of calling."

John Storm laughed, and that provoked her to towering indignation. "Good God, what are you thinking of, man? There's that puir lassie—you're running away from her, too, aren't you? It's shameful, it's disgraceful, it's unprincipled, and *you* to do it too!"

"You needn't trouble about that, auntie," said John; "she is going with me."

"What?" cried Mrs. Callender, and her face expressed boundless astonishment.

"Yes," said John, "you women are brimful of courage, God bless you! and she's the bravest of you all."

"But you'll no have the assurance to tak' that puir bit lassie to yonder God-forsaken spot?"

"She wants to go—at least she wants to leave London."

"What does she? Weel, weel! But didn't I say she was nought but one of your Sisters or sic-like?—And you're going to let a slip of a girl tak' you away frae your ain work and your ain duty—and you call yourself a man!"

He began to coax and appease her, and before long the grim old face was struggling between smiles and tears.

"Tut! get along wi' ye! I've a great mind, though—I'd be liking fine to see her anyway. Now, where does she bide in London?"

"Why do you want to know that, auntie?"

"What's it to you, laddie? Can't a body call to say 'Good-bye' to a lassie, and tak' her a wee present before going away, without asking a man's permission?"

"I shouldn't do it, though, if I were you."

"And why not, pray?"

"Because she's as bright as a star and as quick as a diamond, and she'd see through you in a twinkling. Besides, I shouldn't advise——"

"Keep your advice like your salt till you're asked for it, my man—and to think of any reasonable body giving up his work in London for that—that——"

"Good men have gone out to the mission field, auntie."

"Mission fiddlesticks! Just a barber's chair, fit for every comer."

"And then this isn't the mission field exactly either."

"Mair's the pity, and then you wouldna be running bull-neck on your death before your time."

"None of us can do that, auntie, for heaven is over all."

"High words off an empty stomach, my man, so you can just keep them to cool your parridge. But oh, dear—oh, dear! You'll forget your puir auld Jane Callender, anyway."

"Never, auntie!"

"Tut! don't tell me!"

"Never!"

"It's the last I'm to see of you, laddie. I'm knowing that fine—and me that fond of you too, and looking on you as my ain son."

"Come, auntie, come; you mustn't take it so seriously."

"And to think a bit thing like that can make all this botherment!"

"Nay, it's my own doing—absolutely mine."

"Aye, aye, man's the head, but woman turns it."

They dined together and then got into the carriage for Soho. John talked continually, with an impetuous rush of enthusiasm; but the old lady sat in gloomy silence, broken only by a sigh. At the corner of Downing Street he got out to call on the Prime Minister, and sent the carriage on to the clergy-house.

A newsboy going down Whitehall was calling an evening paper. John bought a copy, and the first thing his eye fell upon was the mention of his own name: "The announcement in another column that Father Storm of Soho intends to take up the work which the heroic Father Damien has just laid down will be received by the public with mingled joy and regret—joy at the splendid heroism which prompts so noble a resolve, regret at the loss which the Church in London will sustain by the removal of a clergyman of so much courage, devotion, independence, and self-sacrifice.... That the son of a peer and heir to an earldom should voluntarily take up a life of poverty in Soho, one of the most crowded, criminal, and neglected corners of Christendom, was a fact of so much significance— —"

John Storm crushed the paper in his hand and threw it into the street; but a few minutes afterward he saw another copy of it in the hands of the Prime Minister as he came to the door of the Cabinet room to greet him. The old man's face looked soft, and his voice had a faint tremor.

"I'm afraid you are bringing me bad news, John."

John laughed noisily. "Do I look like it, uncle? Bad news, indeed! No, but the best news in the world."

"What is it, my boy?"

"I am about to be married. You've often told me I ought to be, and now I'm going to act on your advice."

The bleak old face was smiling. "Then the rumour I see in the papers isn't true, after all?"

"Oh, yes, it's true enough, and my wife is to go with me."

"But have you considered that carefully? Isn't it a terrible demand to make of any woman? Women are more religious than men, but they are more material also. Under the heat of religious impulse a woman is capable of sacrifices—great sacrifices—but when it has cooled— —"

"No fear of that, uncle," said John; and then he told the Prime Minister what he had told Mrs. Callender—that it was Glory's proposal that they should leave London, and that without this suggestion he might not have thought of his present enterprise. The bleak face kept smiling, but the Prime

Minister was asking himself: "What does this mean? Has she *her own* reasons for wishing to go away?"

"Do you know, my boy, that with all this talk you've not yet told me who she is?"

John told him, and then a faint and far-off rumour out of another world seemed to flit across his memory.

"An actress at present, you say?"

"So to speak, but ready to give up everything for this glorious mission."

"Very brave, no doubt, very beautiful; but what of your present responsibilities—your responsibilities in London?"

"That's just what I came to speak about," said John; and then his rapturous face straightened, and he made some effort to plunge into the practical aspect of his affairs at Soho. There was his club for girls and his home for children. They were to be turned out of the clergy-house tomorrow, and he had taken a shelter at Westminster. But the means to support them were still deficient, and if there was anything coming to him that would suffice for that purpose—if there was enough left—if his mother's money was not all gone——

The Prime Minister was looking into John's face, watching the play of his features, but hardly listening to what he said. "What does this mean?" he was asking himself, in the old habitual way of the man whose business it is to read the motives that are not revealed.

"So you are willing to leave London, after all, John?"

"Why not, uncle? London is nothing to me in itself, less than nothing; and if that brave girl to whom it is everything——"

"And yet six months ago I gave you the opportunity of doing so, and then——"

"Then my head was full of dreams, sir. Thank God, they are gone now, and I am awake at last!"

"But the Church—I thought your duty and devotion to the Church——"

"The Church is a chaos, uncle, a wreck of fragments without unity, principle, or life. No man can find foothold in it now without accommodating his duty and his loyalty to his chances of a livelihood. It is a career, not a crusade. Once I imagined that a man might live as a protest against all this, but it was a dream, a vain and presumptuous dream."

"And then your woman movement——"

"Another dream, uncle! A whole standing army marshalled and equipped to do battle against the world's sins toward woman could never hope for victory. Why? Because the enemy is ourselves, and only God can contend against a foe like that. He will, too! For the wrongs inflicted on woman by this wicked and immoral London God will visit it with his vengeance yet. I see it coming, it is not far off, and God help those——"

"But surely, my boy, surely it is not necessary to fly away from the world in order to escape from your dreams? Just when it is going to be good to you, too. It was kicking and cuffing and laughing at you only yesterday——"

"And to-morrow it would kick and cuff and laugh at me again. Oh, it is a cowardly and contemptible world, uncle, and happy is the man who wants nothing of it! He is its master, its absolute master, and everybody else is its wretched slave. Think of the people who are scrambling for fame and titles and decorations and invitations to court! They'll all be in their six feet by two feet some-day. And then think of the rich men who hire detectives to watch over their children lest they should be stolen for sake of a ransom, while they themselves, like human mill-horses, go tramping round and round the safes which contain their securities! Oh, miserable delusion, to think that because a nation is rich it is therefore great! Once I thought the Church was a refuge from this worst of the spiritual dangers of the age, and so it would have been if it had been built on the Gospel. But it isn't; it loves the thrones of the world and bows down to the golden calf. Poverty! Give me poverty and let me renounce everything. Jesus, our blessed Jesus, he knew well what he was doing in choosing to be poor, and even as a man he was the greatest being that ever trod upon the earth."

"But this leper island mission is not poverty merely, my dear John—it is death, certain death, sooner or later, and God knows what news the next mail may bring us!"

"As to that I feel I am in God's hands, sir, and he knows best what is good for us. People talk about dying before their time, but no man ever did or ever will or ever can do so, and it is blasphemy to think of it. Then which of us can prolong our lives by one day or hour or minute? But God can do everything. And what a grand inspiration to trust yourself absolutely to him, to raise the arms heavenward which the world would pinion to your side and cry, 'Do with me as thou wilt, I am ready for anything—anything.'"

A tremor passed over the wrinkles about the old man's eyes, and he thought: "All this is self-deception. He doesn't believe a word of it. Poor boy! his heart alone is leading him, and he is the worst slave of us all."

Then he said aloud: "Things haven't fallen out as I expected, John, and I am sorry, very sorry. The laws of life and the laws of love don't always run together—I know that quite well."

John flinched, but made no protest.

"I shall feel as if I were losing your mother a second time when you leave me, my boy. To tell you the truth, I've been watching you and thinking of you, though you haven't known it. And you've rather neglected the old man. I thought you might bring your wife to me some day, and that I might live to see your children. But that's all over now, and there seems to be no help for it. They say the most noble and beautiful things in the world are done in a state of fever, and perhaps this fever of yours—-H'm. As for the money, it is ready for you at any time."

"There can't be much left, uncle. I have gone through most of it."

"No, John, no; the money you spent was my money—your own is still untouched."

"You are too good, uncle, and if I had once thought you wished to see more of me——"

"Ah, I know, I know. It was a wise man who said it was hard to love a woman and do anything else, even to love God himself."

John dropped his head and turned to go.

"But come again before you leave London—if you do leave it—and now good-bye, and God bless you!"

The news of John Storm's intention to follow Father Damien had touched and thrilled the heart of London, and the streets and courts about St. Mary Magdalene's were thronged with people. In their eyes he was about to fulfil a glorious mission, and ought to be encouraged and sustained. "Good-bye, Father!" cried one. "God bless you!" cried another. A young woman with timid eyes stretched out her hand to him, and then everybody attempted to do the same. He tried to answer cheerfully, but was conscious that his throat was thick and his voice was husky. Mrs. Pincher was at the door of the clergy-house, crying openly and wiping her eyes. "Ain't there lepers enough in London, sir, without goin' to the ends of the earth for 'em?" He laughed and made an effort to answer her humorously, but for some reason both words and ideas failed him.

The club-room was crowded, and among the girls and the Sisters there were several strange faces. Mrs. Callender sat at one end of the little platform, and she was glowering across at the other end, where the Father Superior stood in his black cassock, quiet and watchful, and with the sprawling, smiling face of Brother Andrew by his side. The girls were singing when John entered, and their voices swelled out as they saw him pushing his way through. When the hymn ended there was silence for a moment as if it was expected that he would speak, but he did not rise, and the lady at the harmonium began again. Some of the young mothers from the shelter above had brought down their little ones, and the thin, tuneless voices could be heard among the rest:

There's a Friend for little children

Above the bright blue sky.

John had made a brave fight for it, but he was beginning to break down. Everybody else had risen, he could not rise. An expression of fear and at the same time of shame had come into his face. Vaguely, half-consciously, half-reproachfully, he began to review the situation. After all, he was deserting his post, he was running away. This was his true scene, his true work, and if he turned his back upon it he would be pursued by eternal regrets. And yet he must go, he must leave everything—that alone he understood and felt.

All at once, God knows why, he began to think of something which had happened when he was a boy. With his father he was crossing the Duddon Sands. The tide was out, far out, but it had turned, it was galloping toward them, and they could hear the champing waves on the beach behind. "Run, boy, run! Give me your hand and run!"

Then he resumed the current of his former thoughts. "What was I thinking about?" he asked himself; and when he remembered, he thought, "I will give my hand to the heavenly Father and go on without fear." At the second verse he rallied, rose to his feet, and joined in the singing. It was said afterward that his deep voice rang out above all the other voices, and that he sang in rapid and irregular time, going faster and faster at every line.

They had reached the last verse but one, when he saw a young girl crushing her way toward him with a letter. She was smiling, and seemed proud to render him this service. He was about to lay the letter aside when he glanced at it, and then he could not put it down. It was marked "Urgent," and the address was in Glory's handwriting. The champing waves were in his ears again. They were coming on and on.

A presentiment of evil crept over him and he opened the letter and read it. Then his life fell to wreck in a moment. Its nullity, its hopelessness, its futility, its folly, the world with its elusive joys, love with its deceptions so cruel and so sweet-all, all came sweeping up on him like the sea-wrack out of a storm. In an instant the truth appeared to him, and he understood himself at last. For Glory's sake he had sacrificed everything and deceived himself before God and man. And yet she had failed him and forsaken him, and slipped out of his hands in the end. The tide had overtaken and surrounded him, and the voices of the girls and the children were like the roar of the waters in his ears.

But what was this? Why had they stopped singing? All at once he became aware that everybody else was seated, and that he was standing alone on the edge of the platform with Glory's letter in his hand.

"Hush! hush!" There was a strained silence, and he tried to recollect what it was that he was expected to do. Every eye was on his face. Some of the strangers opened note-books and sat ready to write. Then, coming to himself, he understood what was before him, and tried to control his voice and begin.

"Girls," he said, but he was hardly able to speak or breathe. "Girls," he said again, but his strong voice shook, and he tried in vain to go on.

One of the girls began to sob. Then another and another. It was said afterward that nobody could look on his drawn face, so hopeless, so full of the traces of suffering and bitter sadness, without wanting to cry aloud. But he controlled himself at length.

"My good friends all, you came to-night to bid me Godspeed on a long journey and I came to bid you farewell. But there is a higher power that rules our actions, and it is little we know of our own future, or our fate or ourselves. God bids me tell you that my leper island is to be London, and that my work among you is not done yet."

After saying this he stood a moment as if intending to say more, but he said nothing. The letter crinkled in his fingers, he looked at it, an expression of helplessness came into his face, and he sat down. And then the Father came up to him and sat beside him, and took his hand and comforted it as if he had been a little child.

There was another attempt to sing, but the hymn made no headway this time, for some of the girls were crying, they hardly knew why, and others were whispering, and the strangers were leaving the room. Two ladies were going down the stairs.

"I felt sure he wouldn't go," said one.

"Why so?" said the other.

"I can't tell you. I had my private reasons."

It was Rosa Macquarrie. Going down the dark lane she came upon a woman who had haunted the outside of the building during the past half hour, apparently thinking at one moment of entering and at the next of going away. The woman hurriedly lowered her veil as Rosa approached her, but she was too late to avoid recognition.

"Glory! Is it you?"

Glory covered her face with her hands and sobbed.

"Whatever are you doing here?"

"Don't ask me, Rosa. Oh, I'm a lost woman! Lord forgive me, what have I done?"

"My poor child!"

"Take me home, Rosa. And don't leave me to-night, dear—not to-night, Rosa."

And Rosa took her by the arm and led her back to Clement's Inn.

Next morning before daybreak the brothers of the Society of the Holy Gethsemane had gathered in their church in Bishopsgate Street for Lauds and Prime. Only the chancel was lighted up, the rest of the church was dark, but the first gleams of dawn, were now struggling through the eastern window against the candlelight on the altar and the gaslight on the choir.

John Storm was standing on the altar steps and the Father was by his side. He was wearing the cassock of the Brotherhood, and the cord with the three knots was bound about his waist. All was silent round about, the city was still asleep, the current of life had not yet awakened for the day. Lauds and Prime were over, the brothers were on their knees, and the Father was reading the last words of the dedication service.

"Amen! Amen!"

There was a stroke of the bell overhead, a door somewhere was loudly slammed, and then the organ began to play:

Holy, Holy, Holy, Lord God Almighty.

The brothers rose and sang, their voices filled the dark place, and the quivering sounds of the organ swelled up to the unseen roof.

Holy, Holy, Holy! Merciful and Mighty,

God in Three Persons, Blessed Trinity!

The Father's cheeks were moist, but his eyes were shining and his face was full of a great joy. John Storm was standing with bowed head. He had made the vows of poverty, chastity, and obedience, and surrendered his life to God.